one ingredient,
4 WAYS

one ingredient,
4 WAYS

Delicious ways to stretch everyday ingredients further

First published in 2010
LOVE FOOD is an imprint of Parragon Books Ltd

Parragon
Queen Street House
4 Queen Street
Bath BA1 1HE, UK

Copyright © Parragon Books Ltd 2010

ISBN: 978-1-4075-9089-9

Printed in China

Cover photography by Charlie Richards
Cover photography styling by Mary Wall
Main ingredient photography by Charlie Richards

Notes for the Reader

This book uses both metric and imperial measurements. Follow the same units of measurement throughout; do not mix metric and imperial. All spoon measurements are level: teaspoons are assumed to be 5 ml, and tablespoons are assumed to be 15 ml. Unless otherwise stated, milk is assumed to be full fat, eggs and individual vegetables are medium, and pepper is freshly ground black pepper.

The times given are an approximate guide only. Preparation times differ according to the techniques used by different people and the cooking times may also vary from those given. Optional ingredients, variations or serving suggestions have not been included in the calculations.

Recipes using raw or very lightly cooked eggs should be avoided by infants, the elderly, pregnant women, convalescents and anyone suffering from an illness. Pregnant and breastfeeding women are advised to avoid eating peanuts and peanut products. Sufferers from nut allergies should be aware that some of the ready-made ingredients used in the recipes in this book may contain nuts. Always check the packaging before use.

No shopping needed!

Focusing on just fifty familiar food items, *one ingredient, 4 ways* shows you how to transform everyday ingredients into knock-out meals. The concept couldn't be simpler. The book offers four clear and concise recipes for each ingredient, and you pick and choose according to what's in your refrigerator, freezer and storecupboard. The recipes demonstrate how incredibly versatile even the most mundane ingredient can be. For example, in the section on frozen peas you have the option of a summery chilled pea soup, a stylish scallop and pea purée, comforting rice and peas, or a classic French recipe for peas and baby onions.

Divided into two straightforward chapters, the book opens with *Keep me cool*, which focuses on wholesome fresh produce kept in the refrigerator or freezer. Here you'll find inspiration for anything from broccoli to blueberries, eggs to bacon, or smoked salmon to minced beef. There's plenty of choice for cheese lovers – from homely Macaroni Cheese to Crispy Parmesan-Coated Sea Bass and Deep-Fried Mozzarella – and even some cool ideas for vanilla ice cream.

Then we move on to *Keep me dry*. Here you'll see how a judiciously stocked storecupboard is key to successful improvisation. Whether it's pasta or rice, canned tomatoes or tuna, nuts or beans, chillies or chocolate, these versatile foods and flavourings are ingredients you can use at a moment's notice for a quick bite or for perking up other dishes. The chapter also includes root vegetables such as potatoes and onions – the backbone of endless satisfying dishes to see you through the week.

This book will inject new life into your cooking. It's perfect for people with action-packed lives but who want to eat well with minimum fuss. Once you get into the swing of it, you'll have no difficulty coming up with smart ideas for what to cook, whether it's a feast for friends, a family meal or a peaceful solo supper. There are dishes to tempt both vegetarians and meat-eaters, as well as child-friendly meals, delectable desserts, cakes and tasty snacks.

Take stock!

In these budget-conscious times, most of us need to make maximum use of the food we buy, and keep waste to a minimum. It makes sense to stock up with only what you need for a given period rather than cramming the cupboard and refrigerator with tempting items that you've bought on the spur of the moment, or obscure ingredients that might come in handy should you ever fancy making that dish you enjoyed so much in Morocco.

What you keep in stock depends of course on whether you live in a bustling city with food shops open round the clock, or the countryside where they are few and far between. It also depends on your cooking habits, how many people you cook for, and whether you have laid-back friends who show up for meals unannounced. Whatever your lifestyle, this book is packed with all-important know-how for rustling up tasty no-fuss meals.

Plan ahead!

However much you may enjoy food shopping, it can be time-consuming. With careful planning, though, heavy-duty shopping for the storecupboard or freezer need only be done now and again, allowing you more time for the fun part – choosing items that really are best freshly bought, such as meat, fish and most fruit and vegetables.

You'll find it much easier to shop if you have a plan in mind. Before you go, check out what you have in your food cupboards, refrigerator and freezer, and take a few minutes to think about meals for the next few days. It's a good idea to go armed with a list – that way unnecessary items won't find their way into your supermarket trolley. If you're keen on fresh produce, try buying smaller quantities more often so you can enjoy it at its peak.

And don't forget the smaller shops. Seek out and enjoy proper butchers, fishmongers, delis and cheese shops. They all offer a cornucopia of superb ingredients, perishable and non-perishable, that will make your cooking stand out from the crowd.

Keep me cool

This chapter covers fresh produce that is best stored in the refrigerator or freezer. These foods have a limited shelf-life and will develop unpleasant flavours and unwelcome or even downright harmful bacteria if not stored correctly.

Many people assume the refrigerator operates at a uniform temperature. The reality is that every refrigerator has cold, cool and humid zones, which in turn are better for different types of food. It's worth investing in a refrigerator thermometer so you can check out the temperature of different zones.

Raw foods like meat, poultry and fish go in the coldest part, which should run at 0–5°C. Keep them properly covered and store below other foods to prevent contamination from drips. Dairy products and eggs are best kept in the cool zone, along with opened jars and bottles labelled 'keep refrigerated'. Wrap cheeses in waxed or greaseproof paper to prevent strong flavours transmitting to other foods. Vegetables and fruit need the humidity of the salad drawer. Keep them loosely wrapped in a paper bag or damp kitchen paper.

It's a good idea to give your refrigerator a weekly cull and chuck out anything that's sprouting whiskers, smelling suspicious or has gone beyond its 'use by' date.

1. Tomatoes

serves 4

280 g/10 oz buffalo mozzarella, drained
    and thinly sliced

8 tomatoes, sliced

20 fresh basil leaves

125 ml/4 fl oz extra virgin olive oil

salt and pepper

serves 8

4 tomatoes, peeled, cored, deseeded
    and finely chopped

8 slices ciabatta, about 1 cm/½ inch
    thick

olive oil, as required

3 large garlic cloves, halved

salt

basil leaves, to garnish

Three-colour salad

Arrange the mozzarella and tomato slices on 4 individual serving
plates and season to taste with salt. Set aside in a cool place for 30
minutes.

Sprinkle the basil leaves over the salad and drizzle with the olive oil.
Season with pepper and serve immediately.

Bruschetta

Put the tomatoes in a nylon sieve over a bowl, sprinkle with salt and leave
to drain. Meanwhile, preheat the grill to high with the grill rack positioned
10 cm/4 inches from the heat.

Brush both sides of the bread slices with olive oil. Place on the rack and
grill for 2 minutes, or until crisp and lightly browned, then turn and grill on
the other side. Remove the toast from the heat and rub one side of each
slice with the garlic, pressing down firmly.

Shake the sieve to remove any moisture from the tomatoes, then divide
them between the toasts. Drizzle with a little more olive oil, scatter with
basil leaves and serve.

3

serves 4

3 tbsp olive oil

2 garlic cloves, finely chopped

10 canned anchovy fillets, drained and chopped

140 g/5 oz black olives, stoned and chopped

1 tbsp capers, drained and rinsed

450 g/1 lb tomatoes, peeled, deseeded and chopped

pinch of cayenne pepper

400 g/14 oz dried spaghetti

salt

2 tbsp chopped fresh flat-leaf parsley, to garnish

Spaghetti alla puttanesca

Heat the oil in a heavy-based frying pan. Add the garlic and cook over a low heat, stirring frequently, for 2 minutes. Add the anchovies and mash them to a pulp with a fork. Add the olives, capers and tomatoes and season to taste with cayenne pepper. Cover and simmer for 25 minutes.

Meanwhile, bring a large heavy-based saucepan of lightly salted water to the boil. Add the pasta, return to the boil and cook for 8–10 minutes, or until tender but still firm to the bite. Drain well and transfer to a warmed serving dish.

Spoon the anchovy sauce into the dish and toss the pasta, using 2 large forks. Garnish with the chopped parsley and serve immediately.

4

serves 4

25 g/1 oz butter

1 tbsp caster sugar

500 g/1 lb 2 oz tomatoes, halved

1 garlic clove, crushed

2 tsp white wine vinegar

salt and pepper

pastry

250 g/9 oz plain flour, sifted

pinch of salt

140 g/5 oz butter

1 tbsp chopped oregano,
   plus extra to garnish

5–6 tbsp cold water

Tomato tarte tatin

Preheat the oven to 200°C/400°F/Gas Mark 6. Melt the butter in a heavy-based pan. Add the sugar and stir over a fairly high heat until just turning golden brown. Remove from the heat and quickly add the tomatoes, garlic and white wine vinegar, stirring to coat evenly. Season with salt and pepper.

Tip the tomatoes into a 23-cm/9-inch cake tin, spreading evenly.

For the pastry, place the flour, salt, butter and oregano in a food processor and process until the mixture resembles fine breadcrumbs. Add just enough water to bind to a soft, but not sticky, dough. Roll out the pastry to a 25-cm/10-inch round and place over the tomatoes, tucking in the edges. Pierce with a fork to let out steam.

Bake in the preheated oven for 25–30 minutes, until firm and golden. Rest for 2–3 minutes, then run a knife around the edge and turn out onto a warmed serving plate.

Sprinkle the tarte tatin with chopped oregano, and serve warm.

2. Garlic

serves 4

2 garlic bulbs, outer papery layers
   removed
3 tbsp water
6 tbsp olive oil
2 fresh rosemary sprigs
1 bay leaf
200 g/7 oz soft goat's cheese
1 tbsp chopped fresh mixed herbs, such
   as parsley and oregano
1 baguette, sliced
salt and pepper
salad leaves, to garnish

serves 4

1.5–2 kg/3 lb 4 oz–4 lb 8 oz
   free-range chicken
½ lemon
40 fat garlic cloves, peeled
2 tbsp olive oil
4 sprigs thyme
2 sprigs rosemary
4 sprigs parsley
1 large carrot, roughly chopped
2 celery sticks, roughly chopped
1 onion, roughly chopped
375 ml/13 fl oz white wine
salt and pepper
crusty bread, to serve

Roasted garlic with goat's cheese

Preheat the oven to 200°C/400°F/Gas Mark 6. Place the garlic in an ovenproof dish. Add the water, half the oil, the rosemary and the bay leaf. Season to taste with salt and pepper. Cover with foil and roast for 30 minutes.

Remove the dish from the oven and baste the garlic with the cooking juices. Re-cover and roast for a further 15 minutes, or until tender.

Meanwhile, beat the cheese in a bowl until smooth, then beat in the mixed herbs. Heat the remaining oil in a frying pan. Fry the bread on both sides for 3–4 minutes, or until golden brown.

Arrange the bread and cheese on serving plates garnished with the salad leaves. Remove the garlic from the oven. Break up the bulbs but do not peel. Divide between the plates and serve immediately. Each diner squeezes the garlic pulp onto the bread and eats it with the cheese.

Chicken with 40 garlic cloves

Preheat the oven to 200°C/400°F/Gas Mark 6. Stuff the chicken with the ½ lemon and 4 of the garlic cloves. Rub the chicken with a little oil and some salt and pepper. In a large casserole dish lay a bed of the remaining garlic cloves, the herbs, carrot, celery and onion, then place the chicken on top. Pour over the remaining oil and add the wine. Cover with a tight-fitting lid, place in the oven and bake for 1¼ hours.

Remove the chicken from the casserole and check that it's cooked by piercing with a skewer. The juices should run clear. Cover and keep warm. Remove the garlic cloves from the dish and reserve.

Place the casserole over a low heat and simmer the juices for 5 minutes to make a gravy. Strain, reserving the vegetables.

Carve the chicken and serve it with the vegetables from the casserole. Squeeze the flesh out of the garlic cloves, spread onto the bread and serve.

3

serves 6

2 garlic bulbs, outer papery layers removed

4 tbsp olive oil, plus extra for drizzling

900 g/2 lb pumpkin or butternut squash

2 tbsp fresh thyme leaves, plus extra to garnish

25 g/1 oz butter

1 large onion, finely chopped

1 tbsp plain flour

1.2 litres/2 pints chicken stock

100 g/3½ oz crème fraîche

salt and pepper

Roasted pumpkin, garlic & thyme soup

Preheat the oven to 190°C/375°F/Gas Mark 5. Take two pieces of foil large enough to wrap a garlic bulb and place a bulb in the middle of each. Pour ½ tablespoon of olive oil over each, season with salt and pepper, wrap and place in a large roasting tin. Peel the pumpkin, then cut into large chunks. Toss the chunks in the remaining olive oil, some salt and pepper and half of the thyme leaves. Place in the roasting tin in a single layer and roast, uncovered, for 1 hour.

Meanwhile, place a large heavy-based saucepan over a medium heat, add the butter and melt. Add the onion and cook, stirring occasionally, until soft. Add the flour and cook it through for 2 minutes. Add the stock, a few spoonfuls at a time to begin with, then add all of it.

When the pumpkin is browned remove it from the oven, add to the stock, bring to a simmer and simmer for 10 minutes. Open the garlic packages and leave to cool. When cool enough to touch, break up the bulbs, place the cloves on a chopping board and squeeze down on each until the softened garlic squeezes out.

Remove the soup from the heat and carefully blend in small batches in a food processor with the garlic and the remaining thyme.

Pour into mugs and drop a spoonful of crème fraîche on top. Drizzle a little oil over each, garnish with thyme and serve.

4

serves 4

1 kg/2 lb 4 oz small waxy potatoes, sliced
2 tbsp olive oil
3 garlic cloves, peeled
150 g/5½ oz bacon lardons
600 ml/1 pint double cream
2 tbsp fresh thyme leaves
200 g/7 oz Brie or Camembert, sliced
salt and pepper
crusty bread, to serve

Potato, bacon & garlic gratin

Preheat the oven to 180°C/350°F/Gas Mark 4.

Cook the potato slices in a large saucepan of lightly salted boiling water for 10–15 minutes until just tender. Drain.

Heat the oil in a large frying pan over a medium heat. Hit the garlic cloves with the back of a sturdy knife to split them and add to the frying pan. Add the bacon lardons and cook for 3–4 minutes until just cooked. Add the potato slices, season and cook for 3–4 minutes. Pour in the cream, add the thyme leaves and stir well.

Transfer the mixture to a gratin dish and top with the cheese slices. Bake in the preheated oven for 20 minutes, or until golden and bubbling. Serve with crusty bread.

3. Blueberries

1

serves 2

2 muffins
2 lean bacon rashers
100 g/4 oz fresh blueberries
2 tsp maple syrup (optional)

Toasted muffins with blueberries & bacon

Preheat the grill to medium–high. Slice the muffins horizontally and place them, cut sides down, on the rack in the grill pan.

Lay the bacon rashers on the rack and cook until the tops of the muffins are toasted and the bacon is lightly cooked on one side.

Turn the muffins and divide the blueberries between the bottom halves. Invert the bacon onto the blueberries, covering them completely. Cook for a further 2 minutes, removing the top halves as soon as they are toasted and the bottom when the bacon is browned and crisp.

Place the muffin bases on warmed plates, drizzle with maple syrup, if liked, and add the muffin tops. Serve at once.

2

makes 12

225 g/8 oz plain flour
1 tsp bicarbonate of soda
¼ tsp salt
1 tsp allspice
115 g/4 oz caster sugar
3 large egg whites
3 tbsp low-fat margarine
150 ml/5 fl oz thick natural yogurt or blueberry-flavoured yogurt
1 tsp vanilla extract
85 g/3 oz fresh blueberries

Blueberry & vanilla muffins

Preheat the oven to 190°C/375°F/Gas Mark 5. Place 12 paper muffin cases in a muffin tin.

Sift the flour, bicarbonate of soda, salt and half the allspice into a large mixing bowl. Add 6 tablespoons of the sugar and mix together well. In a separate bowl, whisk together the egg whites. Add the margarine, yogurt and vanilla extract and mix together well, then stir in the blueberries until thoroughly mixed. Add the fruit mixture to the dry ingredients, then gently stir until just combined. Do not overstir the mixture – it is fine for it to be a little lumpy.

Divide the mixture evenly between the paper cases (they should be about two-thirds full). Mix the remaining sugar with the remaining allspice, then sprinkle the mixture over the muffins.

Bake in the preheated oven for 25 minutes, or until risen and golden. Remove the muffins from the oven and serve warm, or place them on a wire rack to cool completely.

3

makes 9 squares

150 g/5½ oz butter, softened, plus extra for
 greasing

2 eggs

175 g/6 oz golden caster sugar

175 g/6 oz self-raising flour, sifted

90 ml/3 fl oz milk

finely grated zest of 1 lemon

225 g/8 oz fresh blueberries

syrup

4 ripe passion fruit

115 g/4 oz icing sugar, plus extra, sifted,
 for dusting

Blueberry & passion fruit drizzle squares

Preheat the oven to 190°C/375°F/Gas Mark 5. Grease and base-line a
23-cm/9-inch square cake tin.

Whisk the butter, eggs and sugar together until pale and fluffy. Fold in
the flour lightly and evenly. Stir in the milk, lemon zest and 175 g/6 oz
of the blueberries. Spread the mixture into the cake tin and bake in the
preheated oven for 25–30 minutes, until firm and golden brown. Remove
from the oven and leave in the tin.

Meanwhile, make the syrup. Scoop the pulp from the passion fruit
and rub through a sieve. Discard the pips. Place the icing sugar and
passion fruit juice in a saucepan and heat gently, stirring, until the sugar
dissolves.

Prick the warm cake with a fork, and spoon the syrup evenly over
the surface. Leave the cake to cool completely in the tin then cut into
9 squares and decorate with the remaining blueberries.

4

makes about 1.5 kg/3 lb 5 oz

675 g/1 lb 8 oz fresh blueberries
225 ml/8 fl oz freshly squeezed orange
   juice
2 whole star anise
1 cinnamon stick, lightly bruised
500 g/1 lb 2 oz granulated sugar
175 ml/6 fl oz liquid pectin

Spicy blueberry & cinnamon jam

Place the blueberries in a preserving pan with the orange juice. Tie up the spices in a small piece of muslin and add to the pan, then simmer over a gentle heat for 20 minutes, or until very soft.

Add the sugar and cook gently, stirring occasionally, until the sugar has completely dissolved. Bring to the boil and boil for 3 minutes, then remove from the heat and stir in the pectin. Leave to cool slightly.

Discard the spices then pot into warmed sterilized jars and cover the tops with waxed discs.

When completely cold, cover with cellophane or lids, label and store in a cool place.

4. Jalapeño Chillies

1

serves 4

400 g/14 oz potatoes, cut into
   medium-sized chunks

400 g/14 oz skinless salmon fillet

2 tbsp mayonnaise

1 egg, beaten

dash of milk, if needed

2 fresh jalapeño chillies, deseeded and
   finely chopped

1 small bunch fresh coriander leaves

plain flour, for dusting

1 tbsp olive oil

salt and pepper

Salmon & jalapeño fish cakes

Cook the potatoes in a large saucepan of lightly salted boiling water for 15 minutes, or until tender.

Meanwhile, lightly poach the salmon fillet in a saucepan of gently simmering water for 5–6 minutes (if in one piece), or until just cooked but still moist. Alternatively, cut into 4 equal-sized pieces and cook in a microwave oven on medium for 3 minutes, then turn the pieces around so that the cooked parts are in the centre, and cook for a further 1–2 minutes – check after 1 minute; the fish should be barely cooked. Using a fork, flake the flesh into a bowl.

Drain the potatoes, return to the saucepan and, while still warm, roughly mash with a fork, adding the mayonnaise, egg and milk, if needed – the mixture must remain firm, so only add the milk if necessary. Stir in the chillies, coriander leaves and salt and pepper to taste, then lightly mix in the salmon flakes.

With floured hands, form the mixture into 8 small patties. Heat the oil in a large non-stick frying pan over a medium–high heat, add the patties and cook for 5 minutes on each side, or until golden brown. Carefully remove with a fish slice and serve immediately.

2

serves 6

175 g/6 oz tortilla chips

400 g/14 oz canned refried beans,
   warmed

2 tbsp fresh jalapeño chillies, finely
   chopped

200 g/7 oz canned or bottled
   pimentos or roasted peppers,
   drained and finely sliced

115 g/4 oz Gruyère cheese, grated

115 g/4 oz Cheddar cheese, grated

salt and pepper

Nachos with jalapeños & cheese

Preheat the oven to 200°C/400°F/Gas Mark 6.

Spread the tortilla chips out over the base of a large, shallow ovenproof dish or roasting tin. Cover with the warmed refried beans. Scatter over the chillies and pimentos and season to taste with salt and pepper. Mix the cheeses together in a bowl and sprinkle on top.

Bake in the preheated oven for 5–8 minutes, or until the cheese is bubbling and melted. Serve immediately.

3

makes 12

12 fresh jalapeño chillies
2 tbsp sesame seeds
2 tsp ground cumin
2 tsp amchoor (dried mango) powder
2 tbsp chipotle chilles in adobo sauce
2 tsp fresh lime juice
2 tsp water
large pinch of salt

batter

280 g/10 oz gram flour
2 tbsp rice flour
½ tsp ground turmeric
¼ tsp bicarbonate of soda
¼ tsp salt
350 ml/12 fl oz water
vegetable oil, for frying
amchoor powder and salt, for sprinkling

Jalapeño bhajis

Make a slit down the length of the jalapeños and halfway around the tops just under the stems. Carefully open up the jalapeños and remove the seeds and membranes using the back of a small spoon. Place the sesame seeds in a spice grinder and grind to a fine paste. Transfer to a bowl, add the cumin, amchoor powder, chipotles, lime juice, water and salt and mix together.

To make the batter, whisk together the gram flour, rice flour, turmeric, bicarbonate of soda and salt in a medium bowl. Whisk in the water until smooth.

In a medium saucepan, heat 15 cm/6 inches of oil to 180°C/350°F, or until a cube of bread browns in 30 seconds. Coat the inside of each jalapeño with about 1 teaspoon of the filling. Top with a very thin coating of the batter (this prevents the filling from leaking out), then dip the jalapeños in the batter, turning to evenly coat. Remove from the batter, letting any excess drip off.

Place the jalapeños in the oil, one or two at a time, and fry for about 5 minutes, until nicely browned and crisp. Remove with a slotted spoon and place on kitchen paper to drain. Sprinkle with amchoor powder and salt and serve immediately.

4

serves 4

1 small wedge watermelon,
  about 115 g/4 oz

2 blood oranges, or 1 red grapefruit

1–2 fresh jalapeño chillies, deseeded and
  finely chopped

2 tsp honey

55 g/2 oz crystallized ginger, drained, with
  2–3 tsp syrup from the jar reserved

1 tbsp chopped fresh mint

Tropical salsa

Peel and deseed the watermelon and finely chop the flesh.

Put in a bowl. Working over the bowl to catch the juices, peel the
oranges, removing and discarding all the bitter white pith. Separate into
segments, chop the flesh and add to the watermelon.

Add the chillies to the fruit with the honey. Stir well.

Finely chop the ginger and add to the bowl with the ginger syrup. Add
the mint and stir well. Transfer the salsa to a serving bowl. Lightly cover
and leave to stand in a cool place, but not the refrigerator, for 30 minutes
to allow the flavours to develop. Stir again and serve.

5. Beef Mince

serves 4

650 g/1 lb 7 oz fresh beef mince

1 red pepper, deseeded and finely chopped

1 garlic clove, finely chopped

2 small red chillies, deseeded and finely chopped

1 tbsp chopped fresh basil

½ tsp ground cumin

salt and pepper

sprigs of fresh basil, to garnish

hamburger buns, to serve

serves 2

3 tbsp olive oil

3 onions, finely chopped

3 garlic cloves, crushed

2 heaped tsp dried mixed herbs or oregano

450 g/1 lb fresh beef mince

1 large egg, beaten

salt and pepper

2–3 tbsp freshly grated Parmesan or mozzarella cheese, to serve

tomato sauce

400 g/14 oz canned chopped tomatoes

1 tbsp tomato purée

pinch of soft light brown sugar

Beef burgers

Preheat the grill to medium–high. Put the minced beef, red pepper, garlic, chillies, chopped basil and cumin into a bowl and mix until well combined. Season with salt and pepper. Using your hands, form the mixture into 4 burger shapes.

Cook the burgers under the grill for 5–8 minutes on each side, or until cooked through. Garnish with sprigs of basil and serve in hamburger buns.

Meatballs

Heat 2 tablespoons of the oil in a saucepan over a medium heat, add the onions and cook, stirring occasionally, for 5 minutes, or until transparent. Add the garlic and cook, stirring, for a further minute, then stir in the herbs. Transfer half the contents of the saucepan to a bowl and leave to cool slightly.

To make the tomato sauce, add all the sauce ingredients, with a very little salt and pepper to taste, to the saucepan, stir well and bring to a simmer. Simmer for 20–30 minutes, stirring once or twice, until you have a rich sauce. Meanwhile, stir the mince, egg and a very little salt and pepper to taste into the onion mixture in the bowl. Combine thoroughly and then form into 16 small balls.

When the tomato sauce is nearly ready, heat the remaining oil in a non-stick frying pan over a medium–high heat, add the meatballs and cook, turning a few times, for 5–6 minutes, or until golden on all sides and cooked through. Serve with the tomato sauce, with the cheese sprinkled over.

3

serves 4

2 tbsp olive oil

1 tbsp butter

1 small onion, finely chopped

1 carrot, finely chopped

1 celery stick, finely chopped

50 g/1¾ oz mushrooms, diced

225 g/8 oz fresh beef mince

75 g/2¾ oz unsmoked bacon or ham, diced

2 chicken livers, chopped

2 tbsp tomato purée

125 ml/4 fl oz dry white wine

½ tsp freshly grated nutmeg

300 ml/10 fl oz chicken stock

125 ml/4 fl oz double cream

salt and pepper

Bolognese sauce

Heat the oil and butter in a large saucepan over a medium heat. Add the onion, carrot, celery and mushrooms to the pan, then fry until soft. Add the beef and bacon to the pan and fry until the beef is evenly browned.

Stir in the chicken livers and tomato purée and cook for 2–3 minutes. Pour in the wine and season with salt and pepper and the nutmeg. Add the stock. Bring to the boil, then cover and simmer gently over a low heat for 1 hour. Stir in the cream and simmer, uncovered, until reduced.

4

serves 4

2 tbsp olive oil

55 g/2 oz pancetta, chopped

1 onion, chopped

1 garlic clove, finely chopped

225 g/8 oz fresh beef mince

2 celery sticks, chopped

2 carrots, chopped

pinch of sugar

½ tsp dried oregano

400 g/14 oz canned chopped tomatoes

2 tsp Dijon mustard

140 g/5 oz Cheddar cheese, grated

300 ml/10 fl oz shop-bought white sauce

225 g/8 oz dried no pre-cook lasagne sheets

115 g/4 oz freshly grated Parmesan cheese, plus extra for sprinkling

salt and pepper

Lasagne

Preheat the oven to 190°C/375°F/Gas Mark 5. Heat the oil in a large heavy-based saucepan. Add the pancetta and cook over a medium heat, stirring occasionally, for 3 minutes, or until the fat begins to run. Add the onion and garlic and cook, stirring occasionally, for 5 minutes, or until softened.

Add the beef and cook, breaking it up with a wooden spoon, until browned all over. Stir in the celery and carrots and cook for 5 minutes. Season to taste with salt and pepper. Add the sugar, oregano and tomatoes and their can juices. Bring to the boil, reduce the heat and simmer for 30 minutes.

Meanwhile, to make the cheese sauce, stir the mustard and Cheddar cheese into the white sauce.

In a large, rectangular ovenproof dish, make alternate layers of meat sauce, lasagne sheets and Parmesan cheese. Pour the cheese sauce over the layers, covering them completely, and sprinkle with Parmesan cheese. Bake in the preheated oven for 30 minutes, or until golden brown and bubbling. Serve immediately.

6. Chicken Breast

serves 4

2 tbsp olive oil

2 celery sticks, chopped

1 large onion, chopped

2 sprigs fresh thyme

250 g/9 oz carrots, diced

250 g/9 oz parsnips, diced

250 g/9 oz turnips or celeriac, roughly chopped

1.5 litres/2¾ pints fresh chicken stock

3 skinless, boneless chicken breasts, about 175 g/6 oz each, roughly cubed

handful of fresh parsley, chopped

2 tbsp lemon juice

salt and pepper

serves 4

850 ml/1½ pints canned coconut milk

200 ml/7 fl oz chicken stock

2–3 tbsp laksa paste

3 skinless, boneless chicken breasts, about 175 g/6 oz each, sliced into strips

250 g/9 oz cherry tomatoes, halved

250 g/9 oz sugar snap peas, halved diagonally

200 g/7 oz dried rice noodles

1 bunch fresh coriander, roughly chopped

Chicken soup

Pour the olive oil into a large heavy-based saucepan. Add the celery and onion and gently fry for about 15 minutes until soft.

Add the thyme, carrots, parsnips and turnips and cook for a further 5 minutes. Add the stock and chicken, and simmer for about 20 minutes. Check that the vegetables are tender, then add the parsley and lemon juice, check the seasoning and serve.

Chicken laksa

Pour the coconut milk and stock into a saucepan and stir in the laksa paste. Add the chicken strips and simmer for 10–15 minutes over a gentle heat until the chicken is cooked through.

Stir in the tomatoes, sugar snap peas and noodles. Simmer for a further 2–3 minutes. Stir in the coriander and serve immediately.

3

serves 4

3 tbsp olive oil

2 leeks, sliced

2 garlic cloves, sliced

3 skinless, boneless chicken breasts, about 175 g/6 oz each, cut into bite-sized pieces

2 sweet potatoes, peeled and cut into chunks

2 parsnips, scrubbed and sliced

1 red pepper, deseeded and cut into strips

1 yellow pepper, deseeded and cut into strips

250 g/9 oz mixed wild mushrooms, cleaned

400 g/14 oz tomatoes, roughly chopped

300 g/10½ oz cooked white long-grain rice

1 small bunch fresh parsley, chopped

125 g/4½ oz mature Cheddar cheese, grated

salt and pepper

Chicken & Autumn vegetable bake

Preheat the oven to 180°C/350°F/Gas Mark 4.

Heat the oil in a large frying pan over a medium heat, add the leeks and garlic and cook, stirring frequently, for 3–4 minutes until softened. Add the chicken and cook, stirring frequently, for 5 minutes. Add the sweet potatoes and parsnips and cook, stirring frequently, for 5 minutes, or until golden and beginning to soften. Add the peppers and mushrooms and cook, stirring frequently, for 5 minutes. Stir in the tomatoes, rice and parsley and season to taste with salt and pepper.

Spoon the mixture into an ovenproof dish, scatter over the Cheddar cheese and bake in the preheated oven for 20–25 minutes. Serve immediately.

4

serves 4

3 skinless, boneless chicken breasts, about
    175 g/6 oz each

4 tsp Cajun seasoning

2 tsp sunflower oil (optional)

1 ripe mango, peeled, stoned and cut into thick slices

200 g/7 oz mixed salad leaves

1 red onion, thinly sliced and cut in half

175 g/6 oz cooked beetroot, diced

85 g/3 oz radishes, sliced

55 g/2 oz walnut halves

4 tbsp walnut oil

1–2 tsp Dijon mustard

1 tbsp lemon juice

2 tbsp sesame seeds

salt and pepper

Cajun chicken salad with mango & beetroot

Make 3 diagonal slashes across each chicken breast. Put the chicken into a shallow dish and sprinkle all over with the Cajun seasoning. Cover and refrigerate for at least 30 minutes. When ready to cook, brush a griddle pan with the sunflower oil, if using. Heat over a high heat until very hot and a few drops of water sprinkled into the pan sizzle immediately. Add the chicken and cook for 7–8 minutes on each side, or until thoroughly cooked. Remove the chicken and reserve.

Add the mango slices to the pan and cook for 2 minutes on each side. Remove and reserve.

Meanwhile, arrange the salad leaves in a bowl and scatter over the onion, beetroot, radishes and walnut halves. Put the walnut oil, mustard, lemon juice and salt and pepper to taste in a screw-top jar and shake until well blended. Pour over the salad and sprinkle with the sesame seeds. Arrange the mango and the salad on a serving plate and top with the chicken breast and a few of the salad leaves.

7. Bacon

serves 4

450 g/1 lb dried spaghetti

1 tbsp olive oil

225 g/8 oz bacon rashers, chopped

4 eggs

5 tbsp single cream

2 tbsp freshly grated Parmesan cheese

salt and pepper

serves 4

4 tbsp olive oil

4 bacon rashers, diced

1 thick slice white bread, crusts removed, cut into cubes

450 g/1 lb fresh spinach, torn or shredded

Spaghetti carbonara

Bring a large heavy-based saucepan of lightly salted water to the boil. Add the pasta, return to the boil and cook for 8–10 minutes, or until tender but still firm to the bite.

Meanwhile, heat the oil in a heavy-based frying pan. Add the bacon and cook over a medium heat, stirring frequently, for 8–10 minutes.

Beat the eggs with the cream in a small bowl and season to taste with salt and pepper. Drain the pasta and return it to the saucepan. Tip in the contents of the frying pan, then add the egg mixture and half the Parmesan cheese. Stir well, then transfer to a warmed serving dish. Serve immediately, sprinkled with the remaining cheese.

Crispy spinach & bacon salad

Heat 2 tablespoons of the olive oil in a large frying pan over a high heat. Add the diced bacon to the pan and cook for 3–4 minutes, or until crisp. Remove with a slotted spoon, draining carefully, and set aside.

Toss the cubes of bread in the fat remaining in the pan over a high heat for about 4 minutes, or until crisp and golden. Remove the croûtons with a slotted spoon, draining carefully, and set them aside.

Add the remaining oil to the frying pan and heat. Toss the spinach in the oil over a high heat for about 3 minutes, or until it has just wilted. Turn into a serving bowl and sprinkle with the bacon and croûtons. Serve immediately.

3

makes 12

pastry

100 g/3½ oz unsalted butter, chilled and diced, plus extra for greasing

225 g/8 oz plain flour

pinch of salt

½ tsp paprika

filling

25 g/1 oz unsalted butter

1 tsp olive oil

1 leek, trimmed and chopped

8 bacon rashers, cut into lardons

2 eggs, beaten

150 ml/5 fl oz double cream

1 tsp snipped fresh chives

salt and pepper

Leek & bacon tartlets

Lightly grease a 7.5-cm/3-inch, 12-hole muffin tin. Sift the flour, salt and paprika into a bowl and rub in the butter until the mixture resembles breadcrumbs. Add a little cold water to bring the dough together. Knead the dough briefly on a floured work surface.

Divide the pastry in half. Roll out 1 piece of pastry and, using a 9-cm/3½-inch plain cutter, cut out 6 rounds, then roll each round into a 12-cm/4½-inch round. Repeat with the other half of the pastry until you have 12 rounds, then use to line the muffin tin. Cover and chill in the refrigerator for 30 minutes.

Meanwhile, preheat the oven to 200°C/400°F/Gas Mark 6. To make the filling, melt the butter with the oil in a non-stick frying pan over a medium heat, add the leek and cook, for 5 minutes until soft. Remove with a slotted spoon and set aside. Add the lardons to the frying pan and cook until crisp. Remove and drain on kitchen paper.

Line the pastry cases with baking paper and baking beans and bake in the preheated oven for 10 minutes. Whisk the eggs and cream together in a bowl, season to taste with salt and pepper, then stir in the chives with the cooked leek and bacon. Remove the pastry cases from the oven and lift out the paper and beans. Divide the bacon and leek mixture between the pastry cases and bake for 10 minutes until the tarts are golden and risen. Transfer to a wire rack. Serve warm or cold.

4

serves 4

1 tbsp butter

2 garlic cloves, chopped

1 onion, sliced

250 g/9 oz bacon rashers, chopped

2 large leeks, sliced

2 tbsp plain flour

1 litre/1¾ pints chicken stock

800 g/1 lb 12 oz potatoes, chopped

200 g/7 oz skinless chicken breast, chopped

4 tbsp double cream

salt and pepper

grilled bacon rashers and sprigs of fresh flat-leaf parsley, to garnish

Chicken & potato soup with bacon

Melt the butter in a large saucepan over a medium heat. Add the garlic and onion and cook, stirring, for 3 minutes, until slightly softened. Add the chopped bacon and leeks and cook for a further 3 minutes, stirring.

In a bowl, mix the flour with enough stock to make a smooth paste, then stir it into the pan. Cook, stirring, for 2 minutes. Pour in the remaining stock, then add the potatoes and chicken. Season with salt and pepper. Bring to the boil, then lower the heat and simmer for 25 minutes, until the chicken and potatoes are tender and cooked through.

Stir in the cream and cook for a further 2 minutes, then remove from the heat and ladle into warmed soup bowls. Garnish with the grilled bacon and flat-leaf parsley, and serve immediately.

8. Smoked Salmon

serves 4

2 tbsp oil

1 large onion, finely chopped

1 large cucumber, peeled, deseeded and sliced

1 small potato, diced

1 celery stick, finely chopped

1 litre/1¾ pints chicken or vegetable stock

150 ml/5 fl oz double cream

150 g/5½ oz smoked salmon slices, finely diced

2 tbsp snipped fresh chives

salt and pepper

serves 4

250 g/9 oz puff pastry

plain flour, for rolling

1 egg, lightly beaten with 1 tbsp milk

1 small red onion, sliced

100 g/3½ oz goat's cheese, crumbled

4 slices smoked salmon

pepper

Cold cucumber & smoked salmon soup

Heat the oil in a large saucepan over a medium heat. Add the onion and cook for about 3 minutes, until it begins to soften.

Add the cucumber, potato, celery and stock, along with a large pinch of salt, if using unsalted stock. Bring to the boil, reduce the heat, cover and cook gently for about 20 minutes until the vegetables are tender.

Allow the soup to cool slightly, then transfer to a food processor or blender, working in batches if necessary. Purée the soup until smooth. (If using a food processor, strain off the cooking liquid and reserve it. Purée the soup solids with enough cooking liquid to moisten them, then combine with the remaining liquid.)

Transfer the puréed soup into a large container. Cover and refrigerate until cold.

Stir the cream, salmon and chives into the soup. If time permits, chill for at least 1 hour to allow the flavours to blend. Taste and adjust the seasoning, adding salt, if needed, and pepper. Ladle into chilled bowls and serve.

Smoked salmon & goat's cheese tarts

Preheat the oven to 200°C/400°F/Gas Mark 6. Roll out the puff pastry to 5 mm/¼ inch thick on a lightly floured work surface and cut into 4 even-sized squares. Place on an ungreased baking tray and brush each square lightly with the egg mixture. Divide the sliced onion evenly between the tarts and top with goat's cheese.

Bake for 20–25 minutes, or until the pastry has risen and is golden brown. Leave to cool slightly, then top with the slices of smoked salmon and season to taste with pepper. Serve immediately.

3

serves 4

350 g/12 oz linguine
2 tbsp olive oil
1 garlic clove, finely chopped
115 g/4 oz smoked salmon slices
55 g/2 oz rocket
salt and pepper

Linguine with smoked salmon & rocket

Bring a large heavy-based saucepan of lightly salted water to the boil. Add the pasta, return to the boil and cook for 8–10 minutes, or until the pasta is tender but still firm to the bite.

Just before the end of the cooking time, heat the olive oil in a heavy-based frying pan. Add the garlic and cook over a low heat for 1 minute, stirring constantly. Do not allow the garlic to brown or it will taste bitter. Add the salmon and rocket. Season to taste with salt and pepper and cook for 1 minute, stirring constantly. Remove the frying pan from the heat.

Drain the pasta and transfer to a warmed serving dish. Add the smoked salmon and rocket mixture, toss lightly and serve.

serves 4

200 g/7 oz fresh asparagus spears
1 large ripe avocado
1 tbsp lemon juice
large handful of fresh rocket leaves
225 g/8 oz smoked salmon slices
1 red onion, finely sliced
1 tbsp chopped fresh parsley
1 tbsp chopped fresh chives

dressing

1 garlic clove, chopped
4 tbsp extra virgin olive oil
2 tbsp white wine vinegar
1 tbsp lemon juice
pinch of sugar
1 tsp mustard

Smoked salmon salad with avocado

Bring a large saucepan of lightly salted water to the boil. Add the asparagus and cook for 4 minutes, then drain. Refresh under cold running water and drain again. Set aside to cool.

To make the dressing, combine all the ingredients in a small bowl and stir together well. Cut the avocado in half lengthways, then remove and discard the stone and skin. Cut the flesh into bite-sized pieces and brush with lemon juice to prevent discoloration.

To assemble the salad, arrange the rocket leaves on individual serving plates and top with the asparagus and avocado. Cut the smoked salmon into strips and scatter over the top of the salad, then scatter over the onion and herbs. Drizzle over the dressing and serve.

9. Prawns

serves 4

150 g/5½ oz butter

8 large garlic cloves, finely chopped

1 kg/2 lb 4 oz cooked prawns, shell on

large handful of fresh flat-leaf parsley, finely chopped

salt and pepper

crusty bread, to serve

makes 4

1 ripe avocado

200 g/7 oz cooked peeled prawns

4 x 25-cm/10-inch wraps

4 baby gem lettuce leaves

dressing

3 tbsp mayonnaise

1 tbsp tomato ketchup

1 tsp Worcestershire sauce

dash of Tabasco sauce

salt and pepper

Garlic prawns

Place a large frying pan over a low heat and add the butter. When the butter has melted, add the garlic and gently fry for 5 minutes, stirring occasionally.

When the garlic is starting to brown, add the prawns and gently stir them through the butter. Increase the heat to medium, cover and cook, shaking the pan occasionally for 3 minutes. Add the parsley and cook for a further 2 minutes. Add lots of salt and pepper and transfer to a large bowl.

Transfer the garlic prawns to serving bowls with a large bowl for empty shells. Serve with crusty bread.

Prawn & avocado wraps

Cut the avocado in half, remove the skin and stone and cut the flesh into 8 pieces. To make the dressing, mix the mayonnaise, tomato ketchup, Worcestershire sauce and Tabasco sauce, together in a bowl. Season with salt and pepper, add the prawns and mix again.

Preheat a non-stick pan or grill pan until almost smoking, then cook the wraps one at a time on both sides for 10 seconds. This will add some colour and also soften the wraps.

Place a lettuce leaf in the middle of each wrap and divide the prawn mixture between the wraps. Top with avocado, and then fold in at the ends. Roll up, cut in half and serve.

3

serves 4

115 g/4 oz cooked peeled prawns
4 spring onions, chopped
55 g/2 oz courgette, grated
4 eggs, separated
few dashes of Tabasco sauce, to taste
3 tbsp milk
1 tbsp sunflower or olive oil
25 g/1 oz mature Cheddar cheese, grated
salt and pepper

Prawn omelette

Pat the prawns dry with kitchen paper, then mix with the spring onions and courgette in a bowl and reserve. Using a fork, beat the egg yolks with the Tabasco sauce, milk and salt and pepper to taste in a separate bowl. Whisk the egg whites in a large bowl until stiff, then gently stir the egg yolk mixture into the egg whites, taking care not to over-mix.

Heat the oil in a large, non-stick frying pan and when hot pour in the egg mixture. Cook over a low heat for 4–6 minutes, or until lightly set.

Preheat the grill to low–medium. Spoon the prawn mixture on top of the eggs and sprinkle with the cheese. Cook under the preheated grill for 2–3 minutes, or until set and the top is golden brown. Serve immediately.

serves 4

½ Webbs lettuce, finely shredded

150 ml/5 fl oz mayonnaise

2 tbsp single cream

2 tbsp tomato ketchup

few drops of Tabasco sauce, or to taste

juice of ½ lemon, or to taste

175 g/6 oz cooked peeled prawns

salt and pepper

paprika, for sprinkling

4 cooked prawns, in their shells, and
    4 lemon wedges, to garnish

thinly sliced buttered brown bread,
    to serve (optional)

Prawn cocktail

Divide the lettuce between 4 small serving dishes (traditionally, stemmed glass ones, but any small dishes will be fine).

Mix the mayonnaise, cream and tomato ketchup together in a bowl. Add the Tabasco sauce and lemon juice and season well with salt and pepper.

Divide the prawns equally between the dishes and pour over the dressing. Cover and leave to chill in the refrigerator for 30 minutes. Sprinkle a little paprika over the cocktails and garnish each dish with a prawn and a lemon wedge. Serve the cocktails with the brown bread, if using.

10. Aubergine

serves 2

groundnut or vegetable oil, for deep-frying,
    plus 2 tbsp

2 aubergines, cut into 2-cm/¾-inch cubes

1 bunch spring onions, roughly chopped

2 garlic cloves, chopped

2 red peppers, deseeded and cut into
    2-cm/¾-inch squares

3 courgettes, thickly sliced

400 ml/14 fl oz canned coconut milk

2 tbsp red curry paste

large handful of fresh coriander, chopped,
    plus extra sprigs to garnish

cooked rice or noodles, to serve

Aubergine curry

Heat the oil for deep-frying in a preheated wok or a deep saucepan
to 180°C/350°F, or until a cube of bread browns in 30 seconds. Add
the aubergine cubes, in batches, and cook for 45 seconds–1 minute
until crisp and brown all over. Remove with a slotted spoon and drain
on kitchen paper.

Heat the remaining 2 tablespoons of oil in a separate preheated wok
or large frying pan, add the spring onions and garlic and stir-fry over
a medium–high heat for 1 minute. Add the peppers and courgettes
and stir-fry for 2–3 minutes. Add the coconut milk and curry paste
and bring gently to the boil, stirring occasionally. Add the aubergines
and coriander, reduce the heat and simmer for 2–3 minutes.

Serve immediately with rice or noodles, garnished with the coriander
sprigs.

serves 2

4 tbsp olive oil

2 onions, finely chopped

2 garlic cloves, very finely chopped

2 aubergines, thickly sliced

3 tbsp chopped fresh flat-leaf parsley

½ tsp dried thyme

400 g/14 oz canned chopped
    tomatoes

175 g/6 oz mozzarella, coarsely
    grated

6 tbsp freshly grated Parmesan
    cheese

salt and pepper

Aubergine gratin

Heat the oil in a flameproof casserole over a medium heat. Add the onion
and cook for 5 minutes, or until soft. Add the garlic and cook for a few
seconds, or until just beginning to colour. Using a perforated spoon,
transfer the onion mixture to a plate.

Cook the aubergine slices in batches in the same flameproof casserole
until they are just lightly browned. Transfer to another plate.

Preheat the oven to 200°C/400°F/Gas Mark 6. Arrange a layer of
aubergine slices in the base of the casserole dish or a shallow ovenproof
dish. Sprinkle with some of the parsley, thyme, salt and pepper. Add
layers of onion, tomatoes and mozzarella, sprinkling parsley, thyme, salt
and pepper over each layer.

Continue layering, finishing with a layer of aubergine slices. Sprinkle
with the Parmesan. Bake, uncovered, in the preheated oven for
20–30 minutes, or until the top is golden and the aubergines are tender.
Serve hot.

3

serves 4

225 g/8 oz dried penne or other short
   pasta shapes
3 tbsp olive oil, plus extra for brushing
2 aubergines
1 large onion, chopped
2 garlic cloves, crushed
400 g/14 oz canned chopped tomatoes
2 tsp dried oregano
55 g/2 oz mozzarella cheese, thinly sliced
25 g/1 oz freshly grated Parmesan cheese
5 tbsp dry breadcrumbs
salt and pepper

Stuffed aubergines

Preheat the oven to 200°C/400°C/Gas Mark 6. Bring a large saucepan of
lightly salted water to the boil. Add the pasta, return to the boil and cook for
8–10 minutes, or until tender but still firm to the bite. Drain, return to the pan,
cover and keep warm.

Cut the aubergines in half lengthways and score around the inside with a
sharp knife, being careful not to pierce the shells. Scoop out the flesh with
a spoon. Brush the insides of the shells with olive oil. Chop the flesh and
set aside.

Heat the remaining oil in a frying pan. Fry the onion over a low heat for
5 minutes, until soft. Add the garlic and fry for 1 minute. Add the chopped
aubergine and fry, stirring frequently, for 5 minutes. Add the tomatoes and
oregano and season to taste with salt and pepper. Bring to the boil and
simmer for 10 minutes until thickened. Remove the pan from the heat and stir
in the pasta.

Brush a baking tray with oil and arrange the aubergine shells in a single layer.
Divide half of the tomato and pasta mixture between them. Scatter over the
slices of mozzarella cheese, then pile the remaining tomato and pasta mixture
on top. Mix the Parmesan cheese and breadcrumbs and sprinkle over the top,
patting lightly into the mixture.

Bake in the preheated oven for about 25 minutes, or until the topping is golden
brown. Serve hot.

serves 6–8

2 aubergines
2 red peppers
4 tbsp olive oil
2 garlic cloves, roughly chopped
grated rind and juice of ½ lemon
1 tbsp chopped fresh coriander
½–1 tsp paprika
salt and pepper
garlic bread, to serve

Aubergine & pepper dip

Preheat the oven to 190°C/375°F/Gas Mark 5. Prick the skins of the
aubergines and peppers with a fork and brush with about 1 tablespoon
of the olive oil. Put on a baking tray and bake in the oven for 45 minutes,
or until the skins are beginning to turn black.

When the vegetables are cooked, put them in a bowl and cover tightly
with a damp tea towel. Leave them for about 15 minutes until they are
cool enough to handle, then cut the aubergines in half lengthways,
carefully scoop out the flesh and discard the skin. Cut the aubergine
flesh into large chunks. Remove and discard the stem, core and seeds
from the peppers and cut the flesh into large pieces.

Heat the remaining olive oil in a large, heavy-based frying pan, add the
aubergine flesh and pepper pieces and fry for 5 minutes. Add the garlic
and fry for a further 30 seconds. Turn all the contents of the frying pan
onto kitchen paper to drain, then transfer to a food processor. Add the
lemon rind and juice, the chopped coriander, the paprika and salt and
pepper to taste, and blend until a speckled purée is formed. Turn the dip
into serving bowls and serve with garlic bread.

11. Button Mushrooms

serves 4–6

50 g/1¾ oz butter

1 onion, chopped

700 g/1 lb 9 oz button mushrooms, roughly chopped

850 ml/1½ pints vegetable stock

3 tbsp chopped fresh tarragon, plus extra to garnish

150 ml/5 fl oz crème fraîche

olive oil, for drizzling

salt and pepper

serves 6

450 g/1 lb button mushrooms

5 tbsp olive oil

2 garlic cloves, finely chopped

squeeze of lemon juice

4 tbsp fresh flat-leaf parsley, chopped, plus extra sprigs to garnish

salt and pepper

crusty bread, to serve

Creamy mushroom & tarragon soup

Melt half the butter in a large saucepan. Add the onion and fry gently for 10 minutes, until soft. Add the remaining butter and the mushrooms and stir-fry for 5 minutes, or until the mushrooms are brown.

Stir in the stock and tarragon and bring to the boil. Reduce the heat and leave to simmer gently for 20 minutes. Transfer to a food processor or blender and process until smooth. Return the soup to the pan.

Stir in the crème fraîche and add salt and pepper to taste. Reheat the soup gently until hot. Ladle into warmed serving bowls, garnish with tarragon, drizzle with a little olive oil and serve immediately.

Sautéed garlic mushrooms

Wipe or brush clean the mushrooms, then trim off the stalks. Cut any large mushrooms in half or into quarters. Heat the olive oil in a large, heavy-based frying pan, add the garlic and fry for 30 seconds–1 minute, or until lightly browned. Add the mushrooms and sauté over a high heat, stirring most of the time, until the mushrooms have absorbed all the oil in the pan.

Reduce the heat to low. When the juices have come out of the mushrooms, increase the heat again and sauté for 4–5 minutes, stirring most of the time, until the juices have almost evaporated. Add a squeeze of lemon juice and season to taste with salt and pepper. Stir in the parsley and cook for a further minute.

Transfer the sautéed mushrooms to a warmed serving dish and serve piping hot or warm, garnished with parsley sprigs. Accompany with chunks or slices of crusty bread for mopping up the garlic cooking juices.

3

serves 4

675 g/1lb 8 oz potatoes, diced
1 tbsp olive oil
2 garlic cloves, crushed
1 green pepper, deseeded and diced
1 yellow pepper, deseeded and diced
3 tomatoes, diced
85 g/3 oz button mushrooms, halved
1 tbsp Worcestershire sauce
2 tbsp chopped fresh basil
salt and pepper
fresh basil sprigs, to garnish

Mushroom, potato & pepper hash

Cook the diced potatoes in a large saucepan of lightly salted boiling water for 7–8 minutes. Drain well and reserve. Heat the olive oil in a large, heavy-based frying pan. Add the potatoes and cook over a medium heat, stirring constantly, for about 8–10 minutes, until browned.

Add the garlic and peppers and cook, stirring frequently, for 2–3 minutes. Stir in the tomatoes and mushrooms and cook, stirring frequently, for 5–6 minutes. Stir in the Worcestershire sauce and basil and season to taste with salt and pepper.

Transfer to a warmed serving dish and garnish with basil sprigs.

4

serves 8

2 tbsp olive oil

24 slices chorizo, each about
    1 cm/½ inch thick (about 100 g/3½ oz)

24 button mushrooms

1 green pepper, grilled, peeled and cut
    into 24 squares

crusty bread, toasted, to serve

Chorizo, mushroom & pepper kebabs

Heat the oil in a frying pan over a medium heat. Add the chorizo and fry for 20 seconds, stirring.

Add the mushrooms and continue frying for a further 1–2 minutes, until the mushrooms begin to brown and absorb the fat in the frying pan.

Thread a green pepper square, a piece of chorizo and a mushroom onto a cocktail stick. Continue until all the ingredients are used. Serve hot or at room temperature with toasted crusty bread.

12. Broccoli

serves 4–6

225 g/8 oz broccoli

55 g/2 oz unsalted butter

1 onion, chopped

25 g/1 oz basmati rice

225 g/8 oz skinless, boneless chicken
   breast, cut into thin slivers

25 g/1 oz plain wholemeal flour

300 ml/10 fl oz milk

450 ml/16 fl oz chicken stock

55 g/2 oz sweetcorn kernels

salt and pepper

serves 6

500 g/1 lb 2 oz broccoli, stems
   trimmed and cut into lengths short
   enough to fit on the crostini

100 ml/3½ fl oz olive oil

1 small bunch wild garlic, rinsed,
   patted dry and chopped

1–2 red chillies, deseeded and finely
   chopped

6 slices country-style bread

salt and pepper

Chicken & broccoli soup

Break the broccoli into small florets and cook in a saucepan of lightly salted boiling water for 3 minutes, drain, then plunge into cold water and reserve.

Melt the butter in a saucepan over a medium heat, add the onion, rice and chicken and cook for 5 minutes, stirring frequently.

Remove the saucepan from the heat and stir in the flour. Return to the heat and cook for 2 minutes, stirring constantly. Stir in the milk and then the stock. Bring to the boil, stirring constantly, then reduce the heat and simmer for 10 minutes.

Drain the broccoli and add to the saucepan with the sweetcorn and salt and pepper to taste. Simmer for 5 minutes, or until the rice is tender, then serve.

Wild garlic & broccoli crostini

Preheat the oven to 190°C/375°F/Gas Mark 5. Cook the broccoli in a saucepan of lightly salted boiling water for 10 minutes, or until just tender. Drain well and set aside.

Heat about one third of the oil in a wok or large frying pan over a high heat, add the wild garlic and chilli and stir-fry for 2 minutes. Add the broccoli, season to taste with salt and pepper and stir-fry for 3–4 minutes until hot and crisp.

Meanwhile, drizzle the remaining oil evenly over the bread slices and bake in the preheated oven for 10 minutes, or until crisp and golden. Divide the broccoli mixture between the crostini, add a grinding of pepper, and serve immediately.

3

serves 4

1 sheet ready-rolled puff pastry

225 g/8 oz small broccoli florets, halved
if necessary

125 g/4½ oz diced pancetta

1 small red onion, sliced

100 g/3½ oz Gorgonzola or Roquefort
cheese, chopped

pepper

toasted pine nuts, to garnish

Broccoli, pancetta & blue cheese galette

Preheat the oven to 200°C/400°C/Gas Mark 6. Place the pastry on a baking sheet and lightly score a line all around, cutting only halfway through, to within 1 cm/½ inch of the edge.

Cook the broccoli in a saucepan of lightly salted boiling water for 4–5 minutes, or until just tender. Drain. Fry the pancetta with the onion, stirring, until golden. Stir in the broccoli and season with pepper.

Spread the filling over the pastry, leaving the border clear. Scatter the pieces of cheese evenly over the top.

Bake in the preheated oven for 25–30 minutes, until the pastry is risen and golden. Garnish with toasted pine nuts.

4

serves 4

pastry

175 g/6 oz plain flour, plus extra for dusting

pinch of salt

1¼ tsp paprika

1 tsp dried thyme

75 g/3 oz margarine

3 tbsp water

filling

100 g/3½ oz cauliflower florets

100 g/3½ oz broccoli florets

1 onion, cut into 8 wedges

2 tbsp butter or margarine

1 tbsp plain flour

6 tbsp vegetable stock

125 ml/4 fl oz milk

85 g/3 oz Cheddar cheese, grated

salt and pepper

paprika, to garnish

Cauliflower & broccoli tart

Preheat the oven to 190°C/375°F/Gas Mark 5. To make the pastry, sift the flour and salt into a bowl. Add the paprika and thyme and rub in the margarine. Stir in the water to bind the ingredients into a dough. Roll out the pastry on a floured surface and use to line an 18-cm/7-inch loose-based flan tin. Prick the base with a fork and line with baking paper. Fill with baking beans and bake in the preheated oven for 15 minutes. Remove the paper and beans and return the pastry case to the oven for 5 minutes.

To make the filling, bring a large saucepan of lightly salted water to the boil, add the cauliflower, broccoli and onion and cook for 10–12 minutes, until tender. Drain and reserve.

Melt the butter in a saucepan. Add the flour and cook, stirring constantly, for 1 minute. Remove from the heat, stir in the stock and milk and return to the heat. Bring to the boil, stirring constantly, and add 55 g/2 oz of the cheese. Season to taste with salt and pepper.

Spoon the cauliflower, broccoli and onion into the pastry case. Pour over the sauce and sprinkle with the remaining grated cheese. Return the flan to the oven for 10 minutes until the cheese is golden and bubbling. Garnish with paprika and serve immediately.

13. Courgettes

serves 10–12

55 g/2 oz butter, diced, plus extra
   for greasing
225 g/8 oz self-raising white flour,
   plus extra for dusting
225 g/8 oz self-raising wholemeal flour
1 tsp salt
1½ tsp mustard powder
225 g/8 oz courgettes, coarsely grated and
   patted dry
140 g/5 oz fresh Parmesan cheese,
   finely grated
1 tsp finely chopped fresh thyme
2 eggs, beaten
about 175 ml/6 fl oz semi-skimmed milk
pepper

Courgette & parmesan bread

Preheat the oven to 190°C/375°F/Gas Mark 5. Grease a baking sheet and set aside. Mix the flours, salt, pepper and mustard powder in a large bowl, then lightly rub in the butter until the mixture resembles breadcrumbs. Stir in the courgettes, Parmesan cheese and chopped thyme. Stir in the eggs and enough milk to form a soft dough.

Turn the dough onto a lightly floured surface and knead lightly, then shape into a 20-cm/8-inch round. Place on the prepared baking sheet, then cut three fairly deep slashes in the top of the loaf using a sharp knife.

Bake in the preheated oven for 40–50 minutes or until well risen and deep golden brown. Transfer to a wire rack and leave to cool. Serve warm or cold in slices, on its own or spread with butter.

makes 20–30

100 g/3½ oz self-raising flour
2 eggs, beaten
50 ml/2 fl oz milk
300 g/10½ oz courgettes
2 tbsp fresh thyme
1 tbsp oil
salt and pepper

Courgette & thyme fritters

Sift the self-raising flour into a large bowl and make a well in the centre. Add the eggs to the well and, using a wooden spoon, gradually draw in the flour. Slowly add the milk to the mixture, stirring constantly to form a thick batter.

Meanwhile, wash the courgettes. Grate the courgettes over a sheet of kitchen paper placed in a bowl to absorb some of the juices. Add the courgettes, thyme and salt and pepper to taste to the batter and mix thoroughly, for about a minute.

Heat the oil in a large, heavy-based frying pan. Taking a tablespoon of the batter for a medium-sized fritter or half a tablespoon of batter for a smaller-sized fritter, spoon the mixture into the hot oil and cook, in batches, for 3–4 minutes on each side.

Remove the fritters with a perforated spoon and drain thoroughly on kitchen paper. Keep the fritters warm in the oven while making the rest. Transfer to serving plates and serve hot.

3

serves 4

55 g/2 oz butter, plus extra for greasing

16 courgettes (about 500 g/1 lb 2 oz total weight)

40 g/1½ oz plain white flour

600 ml/1 pint milk

1 tsp Dijon mustard

115 g/4 oz mature Cheddar cheese, grated

8 fairly thin slices lean smoked or unsmoked cooked ham

40 g/1½ oz fresh white or wholemeal breadcrumbs

salt and pepper

snipped fresh chives or parsley, to garnish

Cheesy courgette & ham gratin

Lightly grease a shallow ovenproof dish and set aside. Cook the courgettes in a saucepan of boiling water for 4–5 minutes or until tender. Drain well, set aside and keep warm.

Meanwhile, melt 40 g/1½ oz of the butter in a separate saucepan, then stir in the flour and cook gently for 1 minute, stirring. Remove the pan from the heat and gradually whisk in the milk. Return to the heat and bring gently to the boil, stirring continuously, until the sauce thickens. Simmer for 2–3 minutes, stirring. Remove the pan from the heat and stir in the mustard and 85 g/3 oz of the cheese. Season to taste with salt and pepper.

Preheat the grill to medium–high. Cut each slice of ham in half crossways, then wrap a half slice of ham around each courgette. Place the ham-wrapped courgettes in a single layer in the prepared dish and pour the cheese sauce evenly over the top to cover.

Mix together the remaining cheese and the breadcrumbs and sprinkle evenly over the cheese sauce. Dot with the remaining butter, then place under the grill for a few minutes until lightly browned and bubbling. Garnish with snipped fresh chives and serve.

4

serves 4

1 tbsp olive oil

1 onion, cut into small wedges

1–2 garlic cloves, crushed

2 eggs

2 egg whites

1 courgette, about 85 g/3 oz, trimmed and grated

2 carrots, about 115 g/4 oz, peeled and grated

2 tomatoes, chopped

pepper

1 tbsp shredded fresh basil, for sprinkling

Courgette, carrot & tomato frittata

Heat the oil in a large non-stick frying pan, add the onion and garlic and sauté for 5 minutes, stirring frequently. Beat the eggs and egg whites together in a bowl then pour into the pan. Using a spatula or fork, pull the egg mixture from the sides of the pan into the centre.

Once the base has set lightly, add the grated courgette and carrots with the tomatoes. Add pepper to taste and continue to cook over a low heat until the eggs are set.

Sprinkle with the shredded basil, cut the frittata into quarters and serve.

14. Frozen Peas

serves 3–4

425 ml/15 fl oz vegetable stock or water

450 g/1 lb frozen peas

55 g/2 oz spring onions

300 ml/10 fl oz natural yogurt or single cream

salt and pepper

to garnish

2 tbsp chopped fresh mint

2 tbsp chopped spring onions or chives

grated lemon rind

serves 4

500 g/1 lb 2 oz frozen peas

2 large handfuls fresh mint leaves, roughly chopped

150 g/5½ oz butter

12 fat scallops, roes attached, if possible, and removed from their shells

salt and pepper

olive oil, for drizzling

Chilled pea soup

Bring the stock to the boil in a large saucepan over a medium heat. Reduce the heat, add the peas and spring onions and simmer for 5 minutes.

Cool slightly, then strain twice. Pour into a large bowl, season to taste and stir in the yogurt. Cover the bowl with clingfilm and refrigerate for several hours or until thoroughly chilled.

To serve, remove from the refrigerator, mix well and ladle into individual soup bowls. Garnish with the chopped mint, spring onions and the grated lemon rind.

Scallop & pea purée

Bring a large saucepan of water to the boil, then add the peas. Bring back to the boil and simmer for 3 minutes. Drain the peas, then put them in a food processor with the mint, two thirds of the butter and a large pinch of salt. Blend to a smooth purée, adding a little hot water if the mixture needs loosening. Taste for seasoning, cover and keep warm.

Pat the scallops dry, then season them well with salt and pepper. Place a large frying pan over a high heat and add the remaining butter. When the butter starts to smoke, add the scallops and sear them for 1–2 minutes on each side. They should be brown and crisp on the outside but light and moist in the middle. Remove the pan from the heat.

Spread a pool of pea purée on each of four warmed plates, and place the scallops on top. Drizzle over a little olive oil, season and serve.

3

serves 4

1 tbsp olive oil

4 tbsp butter

55 g/2 oz pancetta or streaky bacon, chopped

1 small onion, chopped

1.4 litres/2½ pints hot chicken stock

200 g/7 oz risotto rice

3 tbsp chopped fresh flat-leaf parsley

225 g/8 oz frozen peas

55 g/2 oz freshly grated Parmesan cheese

pepper

Rice & peas

Heat the olive oil and half of the butter in a heavy-based pan. Add the pancetta and onion and cook over a low heat, stirring occasionally, for 5 minutes until the onion is soft and translucent, but not brown.

Add the stock to the pan and bring to the boil. Stir in the rice and season to taste with pepper. Bring to the boil, reduce the heat and simmer, stirring occasionally, for 20–30 minutes until the rice is tender.

Add the parsley and frozen peas, and cook for about 8 minutes until the peas are heated through. Stir in the remaining butter and the Parmesan cheese. Transfer to a warmed serving dish and serve immediately with pepper.

4

serves 4

15 g/½ oz unsalted butter
175 g/6 oz whole baby onions
900 g/2 lb frozen peas
125 ml/4 fl oz water
2 tbsp plain flour
150 ml/5 fl oz double cream
1 tbsp chopped fresh parsley
1 tbsp lemon juice
salt and pepper

Peas with baby onions

Melt the butter in a large, heavy-based saucepan. Add the baby onions and cook, stirring occasionally, for 5 minutes. Add the peas and cook, stirring constantly, for a further 3 minutes, then add the water and bring to the boil.

Reduce the heat to low, partially cover and simmer for 10 minutes. Beat the flour into the cream. Remove the pan from the heat, stir in the cream mixture and parsley and season to taste.

Return the pan to the heat and cook, stirring gently but constantly, for about 3 minutes, until thickened. Stir the lemon juice into the sauce and serve the peas immediately.

15. Shortcrust Pastry

serves 4

375 g/13 oz ready-made shortcrust pastry
   butter, for greasing
1 bunch thin asparagus spears
250 g/9 oz spinach leaves
3 large eggs, beaten
150 ml/5 fl oz double cream
1 garlic clove, crushed
10 small cherry tomatoes, halved
handful of fresh basil, chopped
25 g/1 oz freshly grated Parmesan cheese
salt and pepper

makes 12

450 g/16 oz ready-made shortcrust
   pastry
plain flour, for dusting

filling

25 g/1 oz butter
2 celery sticks, finely chopped
1 small leek, trimmed and finely
   chopped
200 ml/7 fl oz double cream,
   plus 2 tbsp extra
200 g/7 oz Stilton cheese
3 egg yolks
salt and pepper

Asparagus & tomato tart

Preheat the oven to 190°C/375°F/Gas Mark 5. Remove the pastry
from the refrigerator at least 15 minutes before use, otherwise it may
be brittle and difficult to handle. Grease a 25–30-cm/10–12-inch
tart tin with butter, then roll out the pastry and line the tin with it. Cut
off any excess, prick the base with a fork and cover with a piece
of greaseproof paper. Fill with baking beans, then blind-bake it for
20–30 minutes until lightly browned. Remove from the oven and
leave to cool slightly. Reduce the oven temperature to 180°C/350°F/
Gas Mark 4.

Meanwhile, bend the asparagus spears until they snap, and discard
the woody bases. Bring a large saucepan of water to the boil, add
the asparagus and blanch for 1 minute, then remove with a slotted
spoon and drain. Add the spinach to the boiling water, then remove
immediately and drain very well.

Mix the eggs, cream and garlic together and season with salt and
pepper. Lay the blanched spinach at the bottom of the pastry base,
add the asparagus and tomatoes, cut side up, in any arrangement
you like, scatter over the basil, then pour the egg mixture on top.
Transfer to the oven and bake for about 35 minutes, or until the filling
has set nicely. Sprinkle the Parmesan cheese on top and leave to
cool to room temperature before serving.

Stilton & leek tartlets

Turn out the pastry onto a floured surface and cut the dough in half. Roll
out the first piece and cut out six 9-cm/3½-inch circles. Take each circle
and roll out to 12 cm/4½ inches diameter and fit into the muffin holes,
pressing to fill the holes. Do the same with the remaining dough. Put a
piece of baking paper in each hole, fill with baking beans then put the tray
in the refrigerator to chill for 30 minutes. Meanwhile, preheat the oven to
200°C/400°F/Gas Mark 6.

Remove the muffin tray from the refrigerator and bake the tartlets blind
for 10 minutes in the preheated oven then carefully remove the paper
and beans. Melt the butter in a frying pan, add the celery and leek and
cook for 15 minutes, until soft. Add 2 tablespoons of the double cream and
crumble in the Stilton, mix well and season with salt and pepper. Bring the
remaining cream to a simmer in another pan, then pour on to the egg yolks,
stirring all the time. Mix in the Stilton mixture and spoon into the pastry
cases. Bake for 10 minutes then turn the tray around in the oven and bake
for a further 5 minutes. Cool in the tin for 5 minutes before serving.

3

serves 8–10

butter, for greasing

plain flour, for dusting

250 g/9 oz ready-made shortcrust pastry

3 tbsp cornflour

85 g/3 oz caster sugar

grated rind of 3 lemons

200 ml/7 fl oz cold water

150 ml/5 fl oz lemon juice

3 egg yolks

55 g/2 oz unsalted butter, cut into small cubes

meringue

3 egg whites

175 g/6 oz caster sugar

1 tsp golden granulated sugar

Lemon meringue pie

Grease a 25-cm/10-inch flan tin. On a lightly floured work surface, roll out the pastry into a circle 5-cm/2-inch larger than the flan tin. Ease the pastry into the tin and press down into the corners. Roll off the excess pastry. Prick the base of the flan and chill, uncovered, in the refrigerator for 20–30 minutes.

Preheat the oven to 200°C/400°F/Gas Mark 6. Line the pastry case with baking paper and fill with baking beans. Bake on a baking tray for 15 minutes. Remove the beans and paper and return to the oven for 10 minutes until the pastry is dry and just colouring. Remove from the oven and reduce the temperature to 150°C/300°F/Gas Mark 2.

Put the cornflour, sugar and lemon rind into a saucepan. Pour in a little of the water and blend to a smooth paste. Gradually add the remaining water and the lemon juice. Place the saucepan over a medium heat and bring the mixture to the boil, stirring continuously. Simmer for 1 minute until smooth and glossy. Remove the saucepan from the heat and beat in the egg yolks, then the butter. Place the saucepan in a bowl of cold water to cool the filling. When cool, spoon the mixture into the pastry case.

To make the meringue, whisk the egg whites using an electric mixer until thick and forming soft peaks. Add the caster sugar, whisking well. The mixture should be glossy and firm. Spoon the meringue over the filling to cover it completely. Swirl the meringue into peaks and sprinkle with the granulated sugar.

Bake for 20–30 minutes until the meringue is crispy and pale gold (the centre should still be soft). Allow to cool slightly before serving.

serves 6

450 g/16 oz ready-made shortcrust pastry

plain flour, for dusting

750 g–1 kg/1 lb 10 oz–2 lb 4 oz cooking
  apples

about 125 g/4½ oz brown or white sugar,
  plus extra for sprinkling

½–1 tsp ground cinnamon

1–2 tbsp water

milk or beaten egg for glazing

custard, to serve

Apple pie

Preheat the oven to 220°C/425°F/Gas Mark 7. Roll out almost two-thirds
of the pastry thinly on a lightly floured surface and use to line a deep pie
plate or shallow pie tin measuring 20–23 cm/8–9 inches in diameter.

Peel, core and slice the apples, then mix them with the sugar and spice
and pack into the pastry case; the filling can come up above the rim. If
the apples are a dry variety add a little water to moisten.

Roll out the remaining pastry to form a lid. Dampen the edges of the pie
rim with water and position the lid, pressing the edges together firmly.
Trim and crimp the edges. Use the pastry trimmings to cut out leaves
or other shapes to decorate the top of the pie. Dampen the shapes and
attach. Glaze the top of the pie with milk or beaten egg, make 1 or 2 slits
in the top to let the steam escape and put the pie on a baking sheet.

Bake in the oven for 20 minutes, then reduce the oven temperature to
180°C/350°F/Gas Mark 4 and cook for 30 minutes, or until the pastry is a
light golden brown. Serve hot or cold with custard, sprinkled with sugar.

16. Cheddar Cheese

1

serves 4

250 g/9 oz dried macaroni pasta
600 ml/1 pint milk
½ tsp grated nutmeg
55 g/2 oz butter, plus extra for cooking
   the pasta
55 g/2 oz plain flour
200 g/7 oz Cheddar cheese, grated
55 g/2 oz freshly grated Parmesan cheese
200 g/7 oz baby spinach
salt and pepper

Macaroni cheese

Cook the macaroni according to the instructions on the packet. Remove from the heat, drain, add a small knob of butter to keep it soft, return to the saucepan and cover to keep warm.

Put the milk and nutmeg into a saucepan over a low heat and heat until warm, but don't boil. Put the butter into a heavy-based saucepan over a low heat, melt the butter, add the flour and stir to make a roux. Cook gently for 2 minutes. Add the milk a little at a time, whisking it into the roux, then cook for about 10–15 minutes to make a loose, custard-style sauce. Add three quarters of the Cheddar cheese and Parmesan cheese and stir through until they have melted in, then add the spinach, season with salt and pepper and remove from the heat.

Preheat the grill to high. Put the macaroni into a shallow heatproof dish, then pour the sauce over. Scatter the remaining cheese over the top and place the dish under the preheated grill. Grill until the cheese begins to brown, then serve.

2

serves 1

1 croissant
2 thin slices cooked ham, halved
mustard (optional)
2 slices Cheddar cheese (about
   25 g/1 oz)
1 egg, hard-boiled and sliced
   (optional)

Ham & cheese croissant

Preheat the grill to a medium–high setting. Slice the croissant horizontally in half, then lay it, cut sides up, on the rack in the grill pan.

Top each croissant half with a slice of cooked ham, overlapping the halves, and spread with a little mustard, if liked. Then top with the slices of cheese, cutting and overlapping them to fit the croissant. Grill, on some foil, for about 2 minutes, until the cheese has melted. The croissant will be warmed through and beginning to brown around the edges.

If including the egg, overlap the slices on the bottom half. Use a knife to scoop any melted cheese off the foil and on to the croissant, then put the top half of the croissant in place. Serve at once.

3

serves 4

1 cauliflower, trimmed and cut into florets
  (675 g/1 lb 8 oz prepared weight)
40 g/1½ oz butter
40 g/1½ oz plain flour
450 ml/16 fl oz milk
115 g/4 oz Cheddar cheese, finely grated
whole nutmeg, for grating
1 tbsp freshly grated Parmesan cheese
salt and pepper

Cauliflower cheese

Cook the cauliflower in a saucepan of boiling salted water for
4–5 minutes. It should still be firm. Drain, place in a hot 1.4-litre/
2½-pint gratin dish and keep warm.

Melt the butter in the rinsed-out saucepan over a medium heat and stir in
the flour. Cook for 1 minute, stirring continuously. Remove from the heat
and stir in the milk gradually until you have a smooth consistency. Return
to a low heat and continue to stir while the sauce comes to the boil and
thickens. Reduce the heat and simmer gently, stirring constantly, for
about 3 minutes until the sauce is creamy and smooth.

Remove from the heat and stir in the Cheddar cheese and a good
grating of the nutmeg. Taste and season well with salt and pepper. Pour
the hot sauce over the cauliflower, top with the Parmesan and place
under a hot grill to brown. Serve immediately.

4

makes 12 biscuits

6 tbsp unsalted butter, chilled, plus extra
   for greasing
4 sun-dried tomatoes (not packed in oil)
350 g/12 oz plain flour
1 tbsp baking powder
½ tsp bicarbonate of soda
½ tsp salt
½ tsp chipotle powder
½ tsp dry mustard
1 tsp dried basil
140 g/5 oz Cheddar cheese, roughly
   grated
175 ml/6 fl oz buttermilk

Cheddar biscuits

Preheat the oven to 200°C/400°F/Gas Mark 6. Grease a baking sheet
and set aside. Soak the sun-dried tomatoes in a small bowl with hot water
to cover for 10 minutes. Drain, squeeze out any excess liquid, and chop
finely. Set aside.

In a large bowl, sift together the flour, baking powder, bicarbonate of
soda and salt. Stir in the chipotle powder, mustard and basil. Cut in
the butter using a pastry blender or rub it in with your fingertips until
completely incorporated. Fold in the cheese and sun-dried tomatoes.
Using a kitchen fork, stir in the buttermilk. The dough will be slightly
sticky. Gather the dough into a ball with your hands and turn out onto a
well-floured work surface. With floured hands, pat the dough to 1 cm/
½ inch thick and cut into 12 squares using a floured knife.

Place the squares on the baking sheet with a little space between
them and bake for about 15 minutes, or until well risen and very lightly
browned. Remove from the oven and serve immediately.

17. Parmesan Cheese

serves 4–6

2 red peppers

4 tbsp olive oil

350 g/12 oz puff pastry, thawed if frozen

plain flour, for dusting

2 ripe but firm tomatoes, thinly sliced

250 g/9 oz ricotta cheese

100 g/3½ oz freshly grated Parmesan
cheese

1 tsp fresh thyme leaves

1 tbsp finely snipped fresh chives

salt and pepper

Summer vegetable & herb tart

Preheat the oven to 200°C/400°F/Gas Mark 6.

Remove the stalks and seeds from the red peppers, and cut the flesh into thin strips. Transfer to a baking tray and drizzle with half the oil. Season to taste with salt and pepper and roast in the preheated oven for 20 minutes, or until soft. Remove from the oven and leave to cool while you prepare the tart case.

Roll out the pastry on a floured work surface and use to line a 23-cm/9-inch tart tin. Prick the base with a fork to prevent the pastry from puffing up.

Scatter the roasted peppers evenly over the base, then arrange the tomato slices on top and season to taste with salt and pepper.

Beat the ricotta cheese in a bowl until smooth, then spoon over the vegetables. Sprinkle over the Parmesan cheese, thyme leaves and chives, then drizzle over the remaining oil. Bake in the preheated oven for 20 minutes, or until the pastry and cheese topping are golden. Serve immediately, or leave to cool.

serves 4

4 sea bass fillets, about 125 g/
4½ oz each, skin on and pin boned

3 tbsp olive oil

juice and grated rind of 1 lemon

100 g/3½ oz freshly grated Parmesan
cheese

1 small bunch fresh parsley, finely
chopped

salt and pepper

green salad, to serve

Crispy parmesan-coated sea bass

Preheat the grill to its highest setting. Brush the grill pan with a little of the oil and lay the fillets in the grill pan, skin-down. Drizzle over a little of the remaining oil, give each fillet a good squeeze of lemon juice and season with salt and pepper.

Mix the lemon rind, Parmesan cheese and parsley together and scatter evenly over the fish. Drizzle over the remaining oil. Cook under the grill for 4 minutes, or until the fish is just cooked and golden – the exact cooking time will depend on the thickness of the fillets. Serve immediately with a green salad and lemon wedges.

3

serves 16

oil, for greasing
140 g/5 oz fine polenta
140 g/5 oz plain flour
4 tsp baking powder
2 tsp celery salt
55 g/2 oz freshly grated Parmesan cheese
2 eggs, beaten
400 ml/14 fl oz milk
55 g/2 oz butter, melted
1 bunch spring onions, chopped
ground black pepper

Spring onion & parmesan polenta bread

Preheat the oven to 190°C/375°F/Gas Mark 5. Grease a 23-cm/9-inch square baking tin. Sift the polenta, flour, baking powder, celery salt and pepper into a bowl and stir in 40 g/1½ oz of the Parmesan cheese. Beat together the eggs, milk and melted butter. Add the egg mixture to the dry ingredients and stir well to mix evenly.

Stir in the chopped spring onions and spread the mixture evenly into the tin. Sprinkle the remaining Parmesan over the mixture. Bake in the preheated oven for 30–35 minutes, or until firm and golden.

makes 12

3 tbsp sunflower oil or 85 g/3 oz butter,
  melted and cooled, plus extra for
  greasing (if using)
280 g/10 oz plain flour
1 tbsp baking powder
½ tsp salt
85 g/3 oz freshly grated Parmesan cheese
60 g/2¼ oz pine kernels
2 eggs
250 ml/9 fl oz buttermilk
pepper

topping
10 g/¼ oz freshly grated Parmesan cheese
35 g/1¼ oz pine kernels

Parmesan & pine kernel muffins

Preheat the oven to 200°C/400°F/Gas Mark 6. Grease a 12-cup muffin tin or line with 12 paper muffin cases.

To make the topping, mix together the Parmesan cheese and pine kernels and set aside.

To make the muffins, sift together the flour, baking powder, and salt and pepper to taste into a large bowl. Stir in the Parmesan cheese and pine kernels.

Lightly beat the eggs in a large jug or bowl then beat in the buttermilk and oil. Make a well in the centre of the dry ingredients and pour in the beaten liquid ingredients. Stir gently until just combined; do not over-mix.

Spoon the mixture into the prepared muffin tin. Scatter the topping over the muffins. Bake in the preheated oven for about 20 minutes, until well risen, golden brown and firm to the touch.

Leave the muffins in the tin for 5 minutes, then serve warm.

18. Mozzarella Cheese

serves 4

2 litres/3½ pints vegetable stock

1 tbsp olive oil

40 g/1½ oz butter

1 small onion, finely chopped

450 g/1 lb risotto rice

55 g/2 oz freshly grated Parmesan cheese

115 g/4 oz mozzarella cheese, diced

1 egg, beaten

115 g/4 oz fresh breadcrumbs

oil, for deep-frying

salt and pepper

salad leaves, to serve

serves 4

1 tbsp butter

4 eggs, lightly beaten

40 g/1½ oz mozzarella cheese, thinly sliced and cut into bite-sized pieces

small handful of baby spinach, stalks removed

salt and pepper

1 oil-cured red pepper, sliced into strips, to garnish

Stuffed rice balls

Bring the stock to the boil in a saucepan, then reduce the heat and keep simmering gently over a low heat while you are cooking the risotto.

Heat the oil with 25 g/1 oz of the butter in a deep saucepan over a medium heat until the butter has melted. Add the onion and cook, for 5 minutes, until softened. Reduce the heat, add the rice and mix to coat in oil and butter. Cook, stirring constantly, for 2–3 minutes, or until the grains are translucent.

Gradually add the hot stock, a ladleful at a time. Stir constantly and add more liquid as the rice absorbs each addition. Cook for 20 minutes, or until all the liquid is absorbed and the rice is creamy but still firm to the bite.

Remove the risotto from the heat and add the remaining butter. Mix well, then stir in the Parmesan cheese. Season to taste with salt and pepper. Leave to cool.

Place 1 heaped tablespoon of the cooled risotto in the palm of your hand. Top with a cube of mozzarella, then place another tablespoon of risotto on top. Press together to form a ball, making sure that the filling is fully enclosed. Chill for 10 minutes, then dip in the beaten egg. Drain and coat in breadcrumbs. Chill for 10 minutes.

Heat enough oil for deep-frying in a large saucepan or deep-fat fryer to 180°C/350°F, or until a cube of bread browns in 30 seconds. Carefully drop the rice balls into the hot oil and cook for 5 minutes, until golden brown. Drain on kitchen paper. Serve with salad leaves.

Mozzarella omelette

Heat a 25-cm/10-inch non-stick pan over a medium–high heat. Add the butter and when it sizzles, pour in the eggs. Season with salt and pepper, then stir gently with the back of a fork until large flakes form. Leave to cook for a few seconds then tilt the pan and lift the edges of the mixture with a spatula, so that uncooked egg flows underneath to cook evenly.

Scatter the cheese and spinach over the top, and leave to cook for a few seconds. Once the surface starts to solidify, carefully fold the omelette in half. Cook for a few seconds, pressing the surface with a spatula. Turn the omelette over and cook for another few seconds, until the cheese is soft and the spinach wilted.

Slip the omelette onto a warm serving dish and slice into segments. Garnish with strips of red pepper before serving.

3

serves 4

2 sfilatini

175 ml/6 fl oz sun-dried tomato purée

300 g/10½ oz mozzarella cheese, drained and diced

1½ tsp dried oregano

2–3 tbsp olive oil

pepper

Cheese & sun-dried tomato toasts

Slice the loaves diagonally and discard the end pieces. Toast the slices on both sides under a preheated grill until golden.

Spread one side of each toast with the sun-dried tomato purée and top with mozzarella. Sprinkle with oregano and season to taste with pepper. Place the toasts on a large baking sheet and drizzle with olive oil.

Bake in a preheated oven, 220°C/425°F/Gas Mark 7, for about 5 minutes, until the cheese has melted and is bubbling. Remove the hot toasts from the oven and leave them to stand for 5 minutes before serving.

4

serves 4

8 slices bread, preferably slightly stale, crusts removed

100 g/3½ oz mozzarella cheese, sliced thickly

50 g/1¾ oz black olives, chopped

8 canned anchovy fillets, drained and chopped

16 fresh basil leaves

4 eggs, beaten

150 ml/5 fl oz milk

oil, for deep-frying

salt and pepper

Deep-fried mozzarella

Cut each slice of bread into 2 triangles. Top 8 of the bread triangles with equal amounts of the mozzarella slices, olives and anchovies. Place the basil leaves on top and season with salt and pepper to taste. Lay the other 8 triangles of bread over the top and press down round the edges to seal.

Mix the eggs and milk together and pour into a dish. Add the sandwiches and leave to soak for about 5 minutes.

Heat the oil in a large saucepan to 180°C/350°F, or until a cube of bread browns in 30 seconds.

Before cooking the sandwiches, squeeze the edges together again. Carefully place the sandwiches in the oil and deep-fry for 2 minutes, or until golden, turning once. (You will have to cook them in batches.) Remove the sandwiches with a slotted spoon and drain on kitchen paper. Serve immediately while still hot.

19. Eggs

1

serves 4

1 clove

2 small shallots, peeled, 1 finely chopped

250 ml/9 fl oz milk

6 black peppercorns

1 bay leaf

25 g/1 oz butter, plus extra for greasing

25 g/1 oz plain flour, plus extra for dusting

4 eggs, whites and yolks separated into separate bowls

½ tsp cayenne pepper

250 g/9 oz cooked crabmeat

Crab soufflé

Preheat the oven to 200°C/400°F/Gas Mark 6. Push the clove into the whole shallot and place in a small saucepan with the milk, peppercorns and bay leaf. Bring to a simmer, then remove from the heat and leave to cool. Strain, reserving the milk and discarding the solids. Grease a 1-litre/1¾-pint high-sided soufflé dish, then dust with flour.

Place a saucepan over a low heat and add the butter and the chopped shallot. Cook for about 5 minutes until the shallot is soft. Add the flour and cook for 3 minutes, stirring, to make a roux. Remove from the heat and add the milk a little at a time, stirring constantly. Add the egg yolks and cayenne pepper and beat with a whisk. Add the crabmeat and warm through. Pour into a mixing bowl.

In a separate bowl, whisk the egg whites until soft peaks form. Add to the crab mixture a quarter at a time, very gently folding through. Spoon into the soufflé dish, place in the preheated oven and bake for 25–30 minutes, until golden on top. Do not open the oven door until the soufflé is cooked. Spoon onto plates and serve.

2

serves 4

2 tbsp olive oil

2 red peppers, deseeded and thinly sliced

2 courgettes, thinly sliced

75 g/ 2¾ oz broccoli florets

4 spring onions, chopped

2 large tomatoes, deseeded and chopped

8 large eggs

3 tbsp freshly grated Parmesan cheese

1 tbsp cold water

salt and pepper

fresh basil leaves, chopped, to garnish

Three-colour frittata

Heat the oil in a large, non-stick frying pan over a high heat, add the red peppers, courgettes and broccoli and cook, stirring, for 3 minutes, or until just softened. Add the spring onions and tomatoes and cook, stirring, for 1 minute. Reduce the heat to medium–low.

Put the eggs, Parmesan cheese and water in a bowl with a little salt and pepper to taste and beat together. Pour the egg mixture evenly over the vegetables in the frying pan. Cook, without stirring, for 6–8 minutes, or until the underside of the frittata is cooked and golden but the top is still runny. Meanwhile, preheat the grill to high.

Put the frying pan under the preheated grill and cook the frittata for 2 minutes, or until the top is cooked and golden, and it is set all the way through. Cut the frittata into 4 wedges, and scatter with basil to garnish.

3

serves 2

4 eggs

100 ml/3½ fl oz single cream

2 tbsp snipped fresh chives, plus 4 whole fresh chives, to garnish

25 g/1 oz butter

4 slices brioche loaf

salt and pepper

Chive scrambled eggs with brioche

Break the eggs into a medium bowl and whisk gently with the cream. Season to taste with salt and pepper and add the snipped chives.

Melt the butter in a sauté pan and pour in the egg mixture. Leave to set slightly, then move the mixture towards the centre of the pan, using a wooden spoon, as the eggs begin to cook. Continue in this way until the eggs are cooked but still creamy.

Lightly toast the brioche slices in a toaster or under the grill and place in the centre of two warmed plates. Spoon over the scrambled eggs and serve immediately, garnished with whole chives.

4

serves 8

500 ml/18 fl oz double cream
1 vanilla pod
100 g/3½ oz caster sugar, plus extra
   for the topping
6 egg yolks

Traditional crème brûlée

Preheat the oven to 160°C/325°F/Gas Mark 3.

Pour the cream into a small saucepan. Split the vanilla pod in half lengthways. Scrape the seeds into the pan, then chop the pod into little pieces and add that too. Bring the cream just to the boil, then reduce the heat and simmer gently for 5 minutes.

Put the sugar and egg yolks in a heatproof bowl and beat with a spoon until well mixed. Pour the hot cream into the egg mixture, beating (not whisking) as you pour, until thickened. Pass this custard through a fine sieve into another bowl or jug. Pour the mixture into a wide, flat dish (or 8 small shallow dishes) and lay in a roasting tray. Boil a kettle and carefully pour the hot water into the tray so that it comes halfway up the sides of the crème brûlée dish (or dishes). Place in the preheated oven and bake for about 35–45 minutes until the custard has just set.

Remove from the oven and leave to cool to room temperature. Sprinkle some caster sugar over the custard and then gently caramelize it using a kitchen blow torch, or under a very hot grill. Leave to cool for a few minutes then serve.

20. Soured Cream

serves 4

675 g/1 lb 8 oz pork fillet

2 tbsp sunflower oil

25 g/1 oz butter

1 onion, chopped

1 tbsp paprika

25 g/1 oz plain flour

300 ml/10 fl oz chicken stock

4 tbsp dry sherry

115 g/4 oz mushrooms, sliced

150 ml/5 fl oz soured cream

salt and pepper

Paprika pork

Cut the pork into 4-cm/ 1½-inch cubes. Heat the oil and butter in a large saucepan. Add the pork and cook over a medium heat, stirring, for 5 minutes, or until browned. Transfer to a plate with a slotted spoon.

Add the chopped onion to the saucepan and cook, stirring occasionally, for 5 minutes, or until softened. Stir in the paprika and flour and cook, stirring constantly, for 2 minutes. Gradually stir in the stock and bring to the boil, stirring constantly.

Return the pork to the saucepan, add the sherry and sliced mushrooms and season to taste with salt and pepper. Cover and simmer gently for 20 minutes, or until the pork is tender. Stir in the soured cream and serve.

serves 6

juice of 1 lime plus extra

3 avocados

2 garlic cloves, chopped

3 spring onions, chopped

2 fresh green chillies, deseeded and chopped

2 tbsp olive oil

1 tbsp soured cream

salt

cayenne pepper, to garnish

tortilla chips, to serve

Guacamole

Put the lime juice into a blender. Halve the avocados and remove the stones. Scoop out the avocado flesh with a spoon and place in a blender.

Add the garlic, spring onions, chillies, olive oil and soured cream and season with salt. Process until smooth. Taste and adjust the seasoning with more salt or lime juice.

Spoon the guacamole into a serving dish. Dust lightly with cayenne pepper and serve with tortilla chips.

3

serves 4–6

6 rashers streaky bacon, rinds removed,
  if necessary
300 g/10 oz soured cream
1 bunch spring onions, finely chopped
4 tbsp snipped fresh chives

Bacon & soured cream dip

Preheat the grill. Place the bacon on the grill rack and cook until well cooked and crisp, turning once. Transfer to kitchen paper to drain and leave to cool.

Put the soured cream in a bowl, then stir in the spring onions and chives. Finely chop the bacon and add it to the bowl and stir together. Transfer to a serving bowl, cover and chill until required.

4

makes 12

3 tbsp sunflower oil or 85 g/
   3 oz butter, melted and cooled,
   plus extra for greasing

2 slices canned pineapple in natural juice,
   plus 2 tbsp juice from the can

280 g/10 oz plain white flour

1 tbsp baking powder

⅛ tsp salt

115 g/4 oz caster sugar

2 medium eggs

200 ml/7 fl oz soured cream

1 tsp vanilla extract

Soured cream & pineapple muffins

Preheat the oven to 200°C/400°F/Gas Mark 6. Grease a 12-cup muffin tin or line with 12 paper cases. Drain and finely chop the pineapple slices. Sift the flour, baking powder and salt into a large bowl. Stir in the sugar and chopped pineapple.

Lightly beat the eggs in a large jug or bowl then beat in the soured cream, oil, pineapple juice and vanilla extract. Make a well in the centre of the dry ingredients and pour in the beaten liquid ingredients. Stir gently until just combined; do not over-mix.

Spoon the mixture into the prepared muffin tin. Bake in the preheated oven for about 20 minutes until well risen, golden brown and firm to the touch. Leave the muffins in the tin for 5 minutes then serve warm or transfer to a wire rack and leave to cool.

21. Vanilla Ice Cream

serves 4

chocolate sauce

55 g/2 oz plain chocolate

4 tbsp golden syrup

15 g/½ oz butter

1 tbsp brandy or dark rum (optional)

sundae

150 ml/5 fl oz double cream

4 bananas, peeled

8 scoops vanilla ice cream

75 g/2¾ oz chopped mixed nuts, toasted

40 g/1½ oz milk or plain chocolate, grated

4 fan wafers, to serve

serves 4

4 tbsp sultanas or raisins

3 tbsp dark rum or ginger wine

4 slices ginger cake

4 scoops vanilla ice cream or
    rum-and-raisin ice cream

3 egg whites

175 g/6 oz granulated or caster sugar

Chocolate banana sundae

To make the chocolate sauce, break the chocolate into small pieces and place in a heatproof bowl with the golden syrup and butter. Set over a saucepan of gently simmering water until melted, stirring until well combined. Remove the bowl from the heat and stir in the brandy, if using.

Whip the cream until just holding its shape and slice the bananas. Place a scoop of ice cream in the bottom of each of 4 tall sundae glasses. Top with slices of banana, some chocolate sauce, a spoonful of cream and a generous sprinkling of nuts.

Repeat the layers, finishing with a good dollop of cream, then sprinkle with the remaining nuts and the grated chocolate. Serve with fan wafers.

Ginger baked alaskas

Preheat the oven to 230°C/450°F/Gas Mark 8. Mix the sultanas with the rum in a small bowl. Place the cake slices, spaced well apart, on a baking tray. Scatter a spoonful of the soaked sultanas over each slice. Place a scoop of ice cream on top of each slice and place in the freezer until solid.

Meanwhile, whip the egg whites in a large bowl until soft peaks form. Gradually whip the sugar into the egg whites, a tablespoonful at a time, until the mixture forms stiff peaks.

Remove the ice-cream-topped cake slices from the freezer and spoon the meringue over the ice cream, spreading to cover the ice cream completely. Bake in the preheated oven for about 5 minutes, until starting to brown.

3

serves 2

350 ml/12 fl oz pineapple juice

90 ml/3¼ fl oz coconut milk

150 g/5½ oz vanilla ice cream

140 g/5 oz frozen pineapple chunks

grated fresh coconut, to decorate

2 scooped-out coconut shells and straws,
    optional, to serve

Coconut cream

Pour the pineapple juice and coconut milk into a food processor. Add
the ice cream and process until smooth.

Add the pineapple chunks and process until smooth. Pour the mixture
into scooped-out coconut shells or tall glasses and decorate with grated
fresh coconut.

Add straws and serve.

4

makes about 30

225 g/8 oz butter, softened
140 g/5 oz golden caster sugar
1 egg yolk, lightly beaten
2 tbsp finely chopped stem ginger, plus
    2 tsp syrup from the jar
250 g/9 oz plain flour
25 g/1 oz cocoa powder
½ tsp ground cinnamon
450 ml/15 fl oz vanilla, chocolate or coffee
    ice cream
salt

Ice cream cookie sandwiches

Put the butter and sugar into a bowl and mix well with a wooden spoon, then beat in the egg yolk, ginger and ginger syrup. Sift together the flour, cocoa powder, cinnamon and a pinch of salt into the mixture and stir until thoroughly combined. Halve the dough, shape into balls, wrap in clingfilm and chill in the refrigerator for 30–60 minutes.

Preheat the oven to 190°C/375°F/Gas Mark 5. Line 2 baking sheets with baking parchment.

Unwrap the dough and roll out between 2 sheets of baking parchment. Stamp out cookies with a 6-cm/2½-inch fluted round cutter and put them on the prepared baking sheets spaced well apart.

Bake for 10–15 minutes, until light golden brown. Leave to cool on the baking sheets for 5–10 minutes, then using a palette knife, carefully transfer to wire racks to cool completely.

Remove the ice cream from the freezer about 15 minutes before serving to allow it to soften. Put a generous scoop of ice cream on half the cookies and top with the remaining cookies. Press together gently so that the filling spreads to the edges. If not serving immediately, wrap the cookies individually in foil and store in the freezer.

Keep me dry

This chapter focuses on all-important storecupboard ingredients – the sauces and condiments that add sparkle to cooking, zesty spices, canned fish, olives, oil, syrups that add sweetness and gloss, and dependable standbys like pasta, rice and beans.

All these goodies can be bought in advance, and many of them stored for weeks or even months until you need them. That said, a well-stocked storecupboard doesn't have to be overflowing. It's far better to have just a few items that get used up and replaced, rather than a vast stash of half-empty jars and bottles that have outstayed their welcome. It also pays to have a well-organized storecupboard, so you won't be rummaging for a mislaid ingredient when you're in the middle of cooking. It's a good idea to decant dry goods into airtight (and pest-proof) containers, away from light, heat and moisture. Add labels so you can easily identify the contents. Check the 'use by' dates often and throw away anything that's past its best.

The chapter also includes apples, onions and potatoes. These should be kept in a dry, cool, airy place rather than the refrigerator – a well-ventilated wicker drawer or vegetable rack is ideal. Keep potatoes away from light, and remove any plastic packaging as this can encourage mould.

22. Bread

serves 4

1 red pepper, cored, deseeded and chopped

1 kg/2 lb 4 oz ripe tomatoes, cored and chopped

2 tbsp very finely chopped onion

3 garlic cloves, crushed

1 cucumber, peeled and chopped

100 g/3½ oz stale bread, crumbled

3 tbsp red wine vinegar or sherry vinegar

3½ tbsp olive oil, plus extra for drizzling

200 g/7 oz ice cubes (optional)

salt and pepper

serves 2

2 tbsp margarine, softened

4 slices of white or brown bread

2 tbsp thousand island dressing

115–175 g/4–6 oz cooked salt beef, thinly sliced

200 g/7 oz bottled sauerkraut, drained

115 g/4 oz Gruyère cheese, grated

vegetable oil, for frying

pickled gherkins, to serve

Gazpacho

Set aside a handful of the red pepper, a handful of the tomatoes and half the chopped onion in the refrigerator. Put the rest of the red pepper and tomato in a food processor with the garlic, cucumber and the remaining onion and purée until smooth. Add the bread, vinegar and oil and whizz again.

Season to taste with salt and pepper. If the soup is too thick, add the ice, then place in the refrigerator for 2 hours.

When ready to serve, check the vinegar and seasoning and ladle into bowls. Scatter over the reserved red pepper, tomatoes and onions, then drizzle over a swirl of olive oil. Serve.

Reuben sandwich

Spread the margarine on one side of each slice of bread and lay margarine-side down. Spread the other sides with 1 tablespoon of the dressing.

Divide the salt beef between 2 slices, tucking in the sides to fit. Divide the sauerkraut and make an even layer on top of the salt beef, before covering with grated cheese. Top with the remaining slices of bread, margarine-side facing up, and press firmly to compress the layers. Heat the oil in a non-stick griddle pan over a medium–high heat and carefully slide the sandwiches into the pan. Using a fish slice, press down on the tops of the sandwiches. Cook for 3 minutes, or until the undersides are crisp and golden. Carefully turn the sandwiches, press down again, and cook for a further 2 minutes, or until the sandwiches are golden, the cheese is melted and the salt beef is hot.

Remove from the heat and transfer the sandwiches to a cutting board. Cut in half and serve with pickled gherkins.

3

serves 4–6

250 g/9 oz stale bread

4 large, vine-ripened tomatoes

about 6 tbsp extra virgin olive oil

4 red, yellow and/or orange peppers

½ cucumber

1 large red onion, finely chopped

8 canned anchovy fillets,
   drained and chopped

2 tbsp capers in brine, rinsed and
   patted dry

about 4 tbsp red wine vinegar

about 2 tbsp balsamic vinegar

salt and pepper

fresh basil leaves, to garnish

Panzanella

Cut the bread into 2.5-cm/1-inch cubes and place in a large bowl. Quarter the tomatoes; reserve the juices. Using a teaspoon, scoop out the cores and seeds and discard, then finely chop the flesh. Add to the bread cubes.

Drizzle 5 tablespoons of the olive oil over the mixture and toss until well coated. Pour in the reserved tomato juice and toss again. Leave to marinate for about 30 minutes. Meanwhile, cut the peppers in half and remove the cores and seeds. Place on a grill rack under a preheated hot grill and grill for 10 minutes, or until the skins are charred and the flesh softened.

Place in a plastic bag, seal, and leave to cool for 20 minutes. Remove the skins, then finely chop. Cut the cucumber in half lengthways, then cut each half into 3 strips lengthways. Using a teaspoon, scoop out and discard the seeds. Dice the cucumber.

Add the onion, peppers, cucumber, anchovy fillets and capers to the bread and toss together. Sprinkle with the red wine and balsamic vinegars and season to taste with salt and pepper.

Drizzle with extra olive oil or vinegar if necessary. Sprinkle the fresh basil leaves over the salad and serve at once.

4

erves 4–6

5 g/3 oz butter, softened
thick slices of white bread
5 g/2 oz mixed dried fruit
  (sultanas, currants and raisins)
5 g/1 oz candied peel
large eggs
00 ml/10 fl oz milk
50 ml/5 fl oz double cream
5 g/2 oz caster sugar
whole nutmeg, for grating
tbsp demerara sugar
cream, to serve

Bread & butter pudding

Preheat the oven to 180°C/350°F/Gas Mark 4.

Use a little of the butter to grease a 20 × 25-cm/8 × 10-inch baking dish and butter the slices of bread. Cut the bread into quarters and arrange half overlapping in the dish.

Scatter half the dried fruit and the candied peel over the bread, cover with the remaining bread slices and add the remaining fruit and peel.

In a mixing jug, whisk the eggs well and mix in the milk, cream and sugar. Pour this over the pudding and leave to stand for 15 minutes to allow the bread to soak up some of the egg mixture. Tuck in most of the fruit so that it does not burn in the oven. Grate the nutmeg over the top of the pudding, according to taste, and sprinkle over the demerara sugar.

Place the pudding on a baking tray and bake at the top of the oven for 30–40 minutes until just set and golden brown.

Remove from the oven and serve warm with a little pouring cream.

23. Pasta

serves 4

- 750 g/1 lb 10 oz mussels, scrubbed and debearded
- 2 tbsp olive oil
- 100 g/3½ oz butter
- 55 g/2 oz rindless streaky bacon, chopped
- 1 onion, chopped
- 2 garlic cloves, finely chopped
- 55 g/2 oz plain flour
- 3 potatoes, thinly sliced
- 115 g/4 oz dried farfalle
- 300 ml/10 fl oz double cream
- 1 tbsp lemon juice
- 2 egg yolks
- salt and pepper
- 2 tbsp finely chopped fresh parsley, to garnish

Mussel & pasta soup

Discard any mussels with broken shells or any that refuse to close when tapped. Bring a large heavy-based saucepan of water to the boil. Add the mussels and oil and season to taste with pepper. Cover tightly and cook over a high heat for 5 minutes, or until the mussels have opened. Remove the mussels with a slotted spoon, discarding any that remain closed. Strain the cooking liquid through a muslin-lined sieve and reserve 1.2 litres/2 pints.

Melt the butter in a clean saucepan. Add the bacon, onion and garlic and cook over a low heat, stirring occasionally, for 5 minutes. Stir in the flour and cook, stirring, for 1 minute. Gradually stir in all but 2 tablespoons of the reserved cooking liquid and bring to the boil, stirring constantly. Add the potato slices and simmer for 5 minutes. Add the pasta and simmer for a further 10 minutes.

Stir in the cream and lemon juice and season to taste with salt and pepper. Add the mussels. Mix the egg yolks and the remaining mussel cooking liquid together, then stir the mixture into the soup and cook for 4 minutes, until thickened.

Ladle the soup into warmed soup bowls, garnish with chopped parsley and serve immediately.

serves 4

- 350 g/12 oz dried macaroni
- 85 g/3 oz butter, plus extra for greasing
- 2 small fennel bulbs, trimmed and thinly sliced
- 175 g/6 oz mushrooms, thinly sliced
- 175 g/6 oz cooked peeled prawns
- pinch of cayenne pepper
- 600 ml/1 pint shop-bought béchamel, or white sauce
- 55 g/2 oz freshly grated Parmesan cheese
- 2 large tomatoes, halved and sliced
- olive oil, for brushing
- 1 tsp dried oregano
- salt

Macaroni & seafood bake

Preheat the oven to 180°C/350°F/Gas Mark 4. Bring a large saucepan of lightly salted water to the boil. Add the pasta, return to the boil and cook for 8–10 minutes, or until tender but still firm to the bite. Drain and return to the saucepan. Add 25 g/1 oz of the butter to the pasta, cover, shake the saucepan and keep warm.

Melt the remaining butter in a separate saucepan. Add the fennel and cook for 3–4 minutes. Stir in the mushrooms and cook for a further 2 minutes. Stir in the prawns, then remove the saucepan from the heat. Stir the cooked pasta, cayenne pepper and prawn mixture into the béchamel sauce.

Grease a large ovenproof dish, then pour the mixture into the dish and spread evenly. Sprinkle over the Parmesan cheese and arrange the tomato slices in a ring around the edge. Brush the tomatoes with oil, then sprinkle over the oregano. Bake in the preheated oven for 25 minutes, or until golden brown. Serve immediately.

3

serves 4

450 g/1 lb asparagus tips
1 tbsp olive oil
225 g/8 oz Gorgonzola cheese, crumbled
175 ml/6 fl oz double cream
350 g/12 oz dried penne
salt and pepper

Penne with asparagus & gorgonzola

Preheat the oven to 230°C/450°F/Gas Mark 8. Place the asparagus tips in a single layer in a shallow ovenproof dish. Sprinkle with the oil and season to taste with salt and pepper. Turn to coat in the oil and seasoning. Roast in the preheated oven for 10–12 minutes until slightly browned and just tender. Set aside and keep warm.

Combine the crumbled cheese with the cream in a bowl. Season to taste with salt and pepper.

Bring a large saucepan of lightly salted water to a boil. Add the pasta, bring back to a boil and cook for 8–10 minutes, or until tender but still firm to the bite. Drain and transfer to a warmed serving dish. Immediately add the asparagus and the cheese mixture. Toss well until the cheese has melted and the pasta is coated with the sauce. Serve immediately.

4

serves 4

3 tbsp olive oil

1 onion, chopped

1 red pepper, deseeded and diced

1 orange pepper, deseeded and diced

800 g/1 lb 12 oz canned chopped
   tomatoes

1 tbsp sun-dried tomato paste

1 tsp paprika

225 g/8 oz pepperoni sausage, sliced

2 tbsp chopped fresh flat-leaf parsley,
   plus extra to garnish

450 g/1 lb dried penne

salt and pepper

Pepperoni & pepper pasta

Heat 2 tablespoons of the oil in a large heavy-based frying pan. Add the onion and cook over a low heat, stirring occasionally, for 5 minutes, or until softened. Add the red and orange peppers, tomatoes and their can juices, sun-dried tomato paste and paprika and bring to the boil.

Add the pepperoni and parsley and season to taste with salt and pepper. Stir well, bring to the boil, then reduce the heat and simmer for 10–15 minutes.

Meanwhile, bring a large heavy-based saucepan of lightly salted water to the boil. Add the pasta, return to the boil and cook for 8–10 minutes, or until tender but still firm to the bite. Drain well. Add the remaining oil and toss. Add the sauce and toss again. Sprinkle with parsley, transfer to a warmed serving dish and serve immediately.

24. Rice

serves 4

55 g/2 oz rice

450 g/1 lb lean minced turkey

1 small cooking apple, peeled, cored and grated

1 small onion, finely chopped

1 garlic clove, finely chopped

1 tsp ground sage

½ tsp dried thyme

½ tsp ground allspice

vegetable oil, for frying

salt and pepper

spring onion and lime, to garnish

Home-made turkey burgers

Cook the rice in a large pan of boiling salted water for about 10 minutes, or until tender. Drain, rinse under cold running water, then drain well again.

Put the cooked rice and all of the remaining ingredients in a large bowl and mix together well. With wet hands, shape the mixture into 8 thick burgers.

Pour a little oil into a large non-stick frying pan, add the burgers and cook for about 10 minutes, turning them over several times, until they are golden brown. Remove from the pan and serve hot, garnished with spring onion and lime.

serves 4

350 g/12 oz rice

2 tbsp vegetable or groundnut oil

2 garlic cloves, finely chopped

2 fresh red chillies, deseeded and chopped

115 g/4 oz mushrooms, sliced

55 g/2 oz mangetout, halved

55 g/2 oz baby sweetcorn, halved

3 tbsp Thai soy sauce

1 tbsp palm sugar or soft, light brown sugar

a few Thai basil leaves

2 eggs, beaten

crispy, fried onions (optional)

Egg-fried rice with vegetables

Cook the rice in a large pan of boiling salted water for about 10 minutes, or until tender. Drain, rinse under cold running water, then drain well again. Set aside to cool.

Heat the oil in a wok or large frying pan and fry the garlic and chillies for 2–3 minutes.

Add the mushrooms, mangetout and baby sweetcorn and stir-fry for 2–3 minutes before adding the soy sauce, sugar and basil. Stir in the rice.

Push the mixture to one side of the wok. Add the eggs to the wok and stir until lightly set before combining with the rice mixture. Transfer to serving plates and top with crispy, fried onions, if using.

3

serves 6

400 g/14 oz rice
2–3 shallots, finely chopped
15 g/½ oz fresh mint leaves, shredded
sweet and sour sauce, to serve

chicken stock

1.7 litres/3 pints water
1 chicken, weighing 900 g–1.1 kg/ 2–2½ lb
25 g/1 oz fresh ginger, peeled and thinly
    sliced
4 spring onions, trimmed and crushed
2–3 tbsp fish sauce

Chicken, mint & shallot rice

For the stock, put the water and chicken in a large saucepan and bring to the boil over a high heat. Reduce the heat to medium–low and add the ginger, spring onions and fish sauce. Simmer for 1½ hours, or until reduced by about half, skimming off any foam.

Transfer the cooked chicken to a platter and separate the meat from the bones and skin. Shred the meat and set aside. Strain the stock, discarding the solids, and remove any fat.

Put the rice in a bowl and cover with cold water. Swirl the rice to loosen any starch and drain. Repeat twice more until the water runs just clear. Transfer the rice to a large saucepan and add 700 ml/1¼ pints of the stock. Cover and bring to the boil over a high heat. Reduce the heat to medium–low and cook for 20–25 minutes, or until the stock is absorbed. Leave for 10 minutes, then fluff up the rice with a fork.

Add the shallots, mint and chicken to the rice and mix well. Serve in individual bowls, drizzled with sweet and sour sauce, to taste.

4

serves 4

115 g/4 oz rice
4 spring onions
225 g/8 oz canned pineapple pieces in natural juice
200 g/7 oz canned sweetcorn, drained
2 red peppers, deseeded and diced
3 tbsp sultanas
salt and pepper

dressing

1 tbsp groundnut oil
1 tbsp hazelnut oil
1 tbsp light soy sauce
1 garlic clove, finely chopped
1 tsp chopped fresh ginger

Tropical rice salad

Cook the rice in a large saucepan of lightly salted boiling water for 15 minutes, or until tender. Drain thoroughly and rinse under cold running water, then drain well again. Place the rice in a large serving bowl.

Using a sharp knife, finely chop the spring onions. Drain the pineapple pieces, reserving the juice in a jug. Add the pineapple pieces, sweetcorn, red peppers, chopped spring onions and sultanas to the rice and mix lightly.

Add all the dressing ingredients to the reserved pineapple juice, whisking well, and season to taste with salt and pepper. Pour the dressing over the salad and toss until the salad is thoroughly coated. Serve immediately.

25. Lentils

serves 4

450 g/1 lb thick, rindless smoked bacon
   rashers, diced

1 onion, chopped

2 carrots, sliced

2 celery sticks, chopped

1 turnip, chopped

1 large potato, chopped

85 g/3 oz puy lentils

1 bouquet garni

1 litre/1¾ pints water or chicken stock

salt and pepper

Bacon & lentil soup

Heat a large heavy-based saucepan or flameproof casserole. Add
the bacon and cook over a medium heat, stirring, for 4–5 minutes,
or until the fat runs. Add the onion, carrots, celery, turnip and potato
and cook, stirring frequently, for 5 minutes.

Add the lentils and bouquet garni and pour in the water. Bring to
the boil, reduce the heat and simmer for 1 hour, or until the lentils
are tender.

Remove and discard the bouquet garni and season the soup to taste
with pepper, and with salt, if necessary. Ladle into warmed soup
bowls and serve immediately.

serves 5

1 tbsp olive oil

1 onion, finely chopped

1 garlic clove, finely chopped

1 carrot, halved and thinly sliced

450 g/1 lb young green cabbage,
   cored, quartered and thinly sliced

400 g/14 oz canned chopped
   tomatoes

½ tsp dried thyme

2 bay leaves

1.5 litres/2¾ pints vegetable stock

200 g/7 oz puy lentils

450 ml/16 fl oz water

salt and pepper

chopped fresh parsley, to garnish

Puy lentil stew

Heat the oil in a large saucepan over a medium heat, add the onion,
garlic and carrot and cook for 3–4 minutes, stirring frequently, until the
onion starts to soften. Add the cabbage and cook for a further 2 minutes.

Add the tomatoes, thyme and 1 bay leaf, then pour in the stock. Bring
to the boil, reduce the heat to low and cook gently, partially covered, for
about 45 minutes until the vegetables are tender.

Meanwhile, put the lentils in another saucepan with the remaining
bay leaf and the water. Bring just to the boil, reduce the heat and
simmer for about 25 minutes until tender. Drain off any remaining water,
and set aside.

Allow the stew to cool, then transfer to a food processor or blender and
process until smooth, working in batches, if necessary. (If using a food
processor, strain off the cooking liquid and reserve. Purée the solids
with enough cooking liquid to moisten them, then combine with the
remaining liquid.)

Return the stew to the saucepan and add the cooked lentils. Taste and
adjust the seasoning, and cook for about 10 minutes to heat through.
Ladle into warmed bowls and garnish with chopped parsley.

3

serves 4

25 g/1 oz puy lentils

1 bay leaf

2 spring onions, finely chopped

50 g /1¾ oz red pepper, deseeded and diced

15 ml/1 tbsp chopped fresh parsley

100 g/3½ oz cherry tomatoes, halved

50 g/1¾ oz rocket

30 g/1⅛ oz goat's cheese, sliced or crumbled

dressing

5 ml/1 tsp olive oil

5 ml/1 tsp balsamic vinegar

2.5 ml/½ tsp runny honey

1 clove garlic, peeled and crushed or finely chopped

Lentil & goat's cheese salad

Rinse the lentils and put in a medium-sized saucepan. Add the bay leaf and cover with plenty of cold water, bring to the boil then reduce the heat and simmer for 20–30 minutes, or until the lentils are tender.

Drain the lentils and transfer to a bowl. Add the spring onions, red pepper, parsley and cherry tomatoes. Mix well.

To make the dressing, whisk together the oil, vinegar, honey and garlic in a bowl and stir into the lentils. Serve on a bed of rocket, with the goat's cheese sprinkled over.

Serves 4–6

2 tbsp olive oil
1 large onion, finely chopped
1 large garlic clove, crushed
½ tbsp ground cumin
½ tsp ground ginger
250 g/9 oz puy lentils
about 600 ml/1 pint vegetable stock
100 g/3½ oz baby spinach leaves
2 tbsp fresh mint leaves
1 tbsp fresh coriander leaves
1 tbsp fresh flat-leaf parsley
lemon juice
salt and pepper
strips of lemon rind, to garnish

Spiced lentils with spinach

Heat the oil in a large frying pan over a medium heat. Add the onion and cook, stirring occasionally, for about 6 minutes. Stir in the garlic, cumin and ginger and cook, stirring occasionally, until the onion starts to brown.

Stir in the lentils. Pour in enough stock to cover the lentils by 2.5 cm/1 inch and bring to the boil. Lower the heat and simmer for 20–30 minutes until the lentils are tender.

Meanwhile, rinse the spinach leaves in several changes of cold water and shake dry. Finely chop the mint, coriander leaves and parsley.

If there isn't any stock left in the pan, add a little extra. Add the spinach and stir through until it just wilts. Stir in the mint, coriander and parsley. Adjust the seasoning, adding lemon juice and salt and pepper. Transfer to a serving bowl and serve, garnished with lemon rind.

26. Extra Virgin Olive oil

serves 4

450 g/1 lb firm ceps

100 ml/3½ fl oz extra virgin olive oil

2 garlic cloves, finely chopped

large handful of parsley, chopped

salt and pepper

sourdough toast, to serve

serves 4

450 g/1 lb dried spaghetti

125 ml/4 fl oz extra virgin olive oil

3 garlic cloves, finely chopped

3 tbsp chopped fresh flat-leaf parsley

salt and pepper

salad, to serve

Ceps with parsley & extra virgin olive oil

Clean the ceps and separate the heads from the stalks. Chop the stalks roughly and set aside. Place a frying pan over a high heat and add the oil. When it's shimmering, add the cep heads and fry. Check the undersides – when they have begun to brown, turn them over. Season with salt and pepper.

Add the garlic, chopped cep stalks and parsley and sauté for 5–10 minutes until the flavours really start to release and the garlic's bite eases a little.

Serve the mushrooms on slices of sourdough toast with a drizzle of the hot olive oil from the pan.

Classic spaghetti olio e aglio

Bring a large heavy-based saucepan of lightly salted water to the boil. Add the pasta, return to the boil and cook for 8–10 minutes, or until tender but still firm to the bite.

Meanwhile, heat the oil in a heavy-based frying pan. Add the garlic and a pinch of salt and cook over a low heat, stirring constantly, for 3–4 minutes, or until golden. Do not allow the garlic to brown or it will taste bitter. Remove the frying pan from the heat.

Drain the pasta and transfer to a warmed serving dish. Pour in the garlic-flavoured oil, then add the chopped parsley and season to taste with salt and pepper. Toss well and serve immediately with salad.

3

serves 4

3 large garlic cloves, finely chopped

2 egg yolks

225 ml/8 fl oz extra virgin olive oil

1 tbsp lemon juice

1 tbsp lime juice

1 tbsp dijon mustard

1 tbsp chopped fresh tarragon

salt and pepper

Aïoli

Ensure that all the ingredients are at room temperature. Place the garlic and egg yolks in a food processor and process until well blended. With the motor running, pour in the oil teaspoon by teaspoon through the feeder tube until the mixture starts to thicken, then pour in the remaining oil in a thin stream until a thick mayonnaise forms.

Add the lemon and lime juices, mustard and tarragon and season to taste with salt and pepper. Blend until smooth, then transfer to a non-metallic bowl.

Cover with clingfilm and refrigerate until required.

makes about 150 ml/5 fl oz

5 g/2 oz fresh basil leaves
garlic clove
5 g/1 oz toasted pine kernels
tbsp extra virgin olive oil
tbsp freshly grated Parmesan cheese
–2 tsp freshly squeezed lemon juice (optional)
alt and pepper

Pesto

Tear the basil leaves roughly into pieces and put in a large mortar with
the garlic, pine kernels and 1 tablespoon of the oil. Pound with a pestle to
form a paste. Gradually work in the remaining oil to form a thick sauce.

Alternatively, put the basil leaves with the pine kernels and a little of the
oil in a food processor and process for 1 minute. Scrape down the sides
of the bowl. With the motor running, gradually add the remaining oil in a
thin, steady stream. Scrape into a bowl.

Add salt and pepper to taste and stir in the Parmesan cheese. If liked,
slacken slightly with the lemon juice.

27. Soy Sauce

serves 4

2 fresh red chillies, deseeded
  and roughly chopped

6 tbsp rice vinegar

1.2 litres/2 pints vegetable stock

2 lemon grass stalks, halved

4 tbsp soy sauce

1 tbsp palm sugar

juice of ½ lime

2 tbsp groundnut or vegetable oil

225 g/8 oz firm tofu (drained weight),
  cut into 1-cm/½-inch cubes

400 g/14 oz canned straw mushrooms,
  drained

4 spring onions, chopped

1 small head pak choi, shredded

Hot & sour soup

Mix the chillies and vinegar together in a non-metallic bowl, cover
and leave to stand at room temperature for 1 hour.

Meanwhile, bring the stock to the boil in a saucepan. Add the lemon
grass, soy sauce, sugar and lime juice, reduce the heat and simmer
for 20–30 minutes.

Heat the oil in a preheated wok, add the tofu cubes and stir-fry over
a high heat for 2–3 minutes, or until browned all over. (You may need
to do this in 2 batches, depending on the size of the wok.) Remove
with a slotted spoon and drain on kitchen paper.

Add the chillies and vinegar with the tofu, mushrooms and half the
spring onions to the stock mixture and cook for 10 minutes. Mix the
remaining spring onions with the pak choi and scatter over the soup
before serving.

serves 4

250 g/9 oz medium egg noodles

2 tbsp sunflower oil

275 g/9¾ oz cooked chicken breasts,
  shredded

1 garlic clove, finely chopped

1 red pepper, deseeded and thinly
  sliced

100 g/3½ oz shiitake mushrooms,
  sliced

6 spring onions, sliced

100 g/3½ oz beansprouts

3 tbsp soy sauce

1 tbsp sesame oil

Chicken chow mein

Place the egg noodles in a large bowl or dish and break them up slightly.
Pour enough boiling water over the noodles to cover and leave to stand
while you prepare the other ingredients.

Heat the sunflower oil in a large preheated wok. Add the chicken, garlic,
red pepper, mushrooms, spring onions and beansprouts to the wok and
stir-fry for about 5 minutes.

Drain the noodles thoroughly. Add the noodles to the wok, toss well and
stir-fry for a further 5 minutes.

Drizzle the soy sauce and sesame oil over the chow mein and toss until
well combined.

Transfer to warmed serving bowls and serve immediately.

3

serves 4

500 g/1 lb 2 oz sweet potatoes

2 garlic cloves, crushed

1 small fresh green chilli, deseeded and chopped

2 fresh coriander sprigs, chopped

1 tbsp dark soy sauce

plain flour, for shaping

vegetable oil, for frying

sesame seeds, for sprinkling

soy-tomato sauce

2 tsp vegetable oil

1 garlic clove, finely chopped

1½ tsp finely chopped fresh ginger

3 tomatoes, skinned and chopped

2 tbsp dark soy sauce

1 tbsp lime juice

2 tbsp chopped fresh coriander

Sweet potato cakes with soy-tomato sauce

To make the soy-tomato sauce, heat the oil in a wok and stir-fry the garlic and ginger over a medium heat for about 1 minute. Add the tomatoes and stir-fry for a further 2 minutes. Remove the wok from the heat and stir in the soy sauce, lime juice and chopped coriander. Reserve and keep warm.

Peel the sweet potatoes and grate finely. Place the garlic, chilli and coriander in a mortar and crush to a smooth paste with a pestle. Stir in the soy sauce and mix with the sweet potatoes.

Put some flour on a plate. Divide the mixture into 12 equal portions, toss each portion in the flour until coated and pat into a flat, round shape.

Heat a shallow layer of oil in a wide frying pan. Fry the sweet potato cakes, in batches, over a high heat until golden, turning once.

Drain the sweet potato cakes on kitchen paper, transfer to a warm serving dish, sprinkle with sesame seeds and serve hot, with the soy-tomato sauce.

4

Serves 4

225 g/8 oz firm tofu (drained weight),
  cut into cubes
250 g/9 oz medium egg noodles
1 tbsp groundnut oil or vegetable oil
1 red pepper, deseeded and sliced
225 g/8 oz broccoli florets
175 g/6 oz baby sweetcorn, halved
  lengthways
2–3 tbsp water
2 spring onions, finely sliced
salt

marinade
1 garlic clove, finely chopped
2.5-cm/1-inch piece fresh ginger, peeled
  and grated
1 tsp sesame oil
1 tbsp clear honey
2 tbsp dark soy sauce

Vegetables with Chinese noodles

Mix together the ingredients for the marinade in a shallow dish. Add the
tofu and spoon the over. Refrigerate for 1 hour to marinate, turning the
tofu occasionally to allow the flavours to infuse.

Preheat the oven to 200°C/400°F/Gas Mark 6. Using a slotted spoon,
remove the tofu from the marinade and reserve the liquid. Arrange the
tofu on a baking sheet and roast for 20 minutes, turning occasionally,
until the tofu pieces are golden and crisp on all sides.

Meanwhile, cook the noodles according to the instructions on the packet,
until tender, then drain. Rinse the noodles under cold running water and
drain again.

Heat a wok or heavy-based frying pan, then add the oil. Add the pepper,
broccoli and sweetcorn and stir-fry, tossing and stirring constantly, over a
medium–high heat for 5–8 minutes or until the vegetables have softened.
Add the water and continue to stir-fry until the vegetables are just tender
but remain slightly crunchy.

Stir in the marinade, noodles, tofu and spring onions and stir-fry until
heated through. Serve immediately.

28. Red Wine

serves 4–6

about 5 tbsp rapeseed or sunflower oil

2 kg/4 lb 8 oz bone-in beef short ribs,
    cut into 10-cm/4-inch pieces

1 large onion, chopped

1 large carrot, peeled and chopped

1 celery stick, chopped

1 bottle red wine

1 litre/1¾ pints beef stock

1 bouquet garni of parsley, thyme and a
    bay leaf

4 tbsp butter

700 g/1 lb 9 oz field mushrooms, wiped
    and thickly sliced

1 tbsp fresh thyme leaves, or ½ tbsp dried
    thyme leaves

salt and pepper

chopped fresh parsley, to garnish

Red wine-braised beef

Preheat the oven to 160°C/325°F/Gas Mark 3. Heat the oil in a large
flameproof casserole over a medium–high heat. Brown the ribs on
all sides in batches, adding more oil if necessary, then remove from
the casserole and set aside. Add the onion, carrot and celery to the
casserole and fry for 5 minutes, until tender. Spoon off any excess
fat. Pour in the wine and stock and bring to the boil.

Reduce the heat and return the ribs to the casserole with the
bouquet garni, salt and pepper to taste and enough water to cover.
Scrunch a piece of foil on top, cover and return to the boil. Cook in
the preheated oven for 1½ hours, until the ribs are just tender. Do
not overcook.

Skim the fat from the surface, remove the ribs and strain the liquid.
Return the ribs and liquid to the casserole and set aside.

Melt the butter with 1 tablespoon of the oil in a large frying pan. Add
the mushrooms and stir for 2 minutes. Add the thyme and salt and
pepper to taste, then stir for a further 3 minutes, until the mushrooms
give off their liquid.

Stir the mushrooms into the casserole. Place over a medium–high
heat and leave to bubble slightly, uncovered, for 45 minutes, until
the sauce is reduced and thick. Remove any loose bones. Adjust the
seasoning, sprinkle with parsley and serve.

serves 4

4 duck portions, about 150 g/5½ oz
    each

1–2 tsp olive oil, plus 1 tbsp (optional)

1 red onion, cut into wedges

2–3 garlic cloves, chopped

1 large carrot, chopped

2 celery sticks, chopped

2 tbsp plain flour

300 ml/10 fl oz red wine

150–200 ml/5–7 fl oz stock or water

7.5-cm/3-inch strip of orange rind

2 tsp redcurrant jelly

115 g/4 oz sugarsnap peas

115 g/4 oz button mushrooms

salt and pepper

Duck & red wine casserole

Remove and discard the fat from the duck. Lightly rinse and pat dry with
kitchen paper.

Heat a large, deep frying pan for 1 minute until warm but not piping hot.
Put the duck portions in the frying pan and heat gently until the fat starts
to run. Increase the heat a little, then cook, turning over halfway through,
for 5 minutes, or until browned on both sides and sealed. Using a slotted
spoon, transfer to a flameproof casserole.

Add 1 tablespoon of the oil if there is little duck fat in the frying pan and
cook the onion, garlic, carrot and celery, stirring frequently, for 5 minutes,
or until softened. Sprinkle in the flour and cook, stirring constantly,
for 2 minutes, then remove the frying pan from the heat.

Gradually stir in the wine and stock, then return to the heat and bring
to the boil, stirring. Season to taste with salt and pepper, then add the
orange rind and redcurrant jelly. Pour over the duck portions in the
casserole, cover and simmer, stirring occasionally, for 1–1¼ hours.

Cook the sugar snap peas in a saucepan of boiling water for 3 minutes,
then drain and add to the casserole. Meanwhile, heat 1–2 teaspoons
of the olive oil in a small saucepan and cook the mushrooms, stirring
frequently, for 3 minutes, or until beginning to soften. Add to the stew.
Cook the stew for a further 5 minutes, or until the duck is tender. Serve
immediately.

3

serves 4

grated rind and juice of 1 orange

300 ml/10 fl oz red wine

3 tbsp clear honey

1 cinnamon stick

1 vanilla pod

½ tsp mixed spice

1 clove

4 firm, ripe pears

½ tsp arrowroot or potato flour

whipped cream, to serve (optional)

Pears in red wine sauce

Bring a saucepan of water to the boil. Meanwhile, put the orange rind and juice, wine, honey, cinnamon stick, vanilla pod, spice and clove in a saucepan and bring to the boil, stirring frequently, then remove the pan from the heat.

Peel the pears, leaving the stem intact, and cut off a small slice from the base so that they will stand upright. Put them into a heatproof bowl and pour the wine mixture over them. Cover the bowl with a sheet of foil and tie in place with kitchen string.

Put the bowl into a steamer and cover with a tight-fitting lid. Set the steamer over the pan of wine and steam for 35–40 minutes, until the pears are tender.

Remove the bowl from the steamer and leave to cool completely. Transfer the pears to a serving dish, standing them upright. Remove and discard the cinnamon stick, vanilla pod and clove from the wine mixture and pour it into a small saucepan. Bring to the boil and cook until reduced to about 150 ml/ 5 fl oz. Reduce the heat to a simmer.

Put the arrowroot into a small bowl and stir in 2 tablespoons of the wine sauce to make a paste. Stir the paste into the pan and simmer gently, stirring constantly, for 2 minutes, until the sauce has thickened. Remove the pan from the heat and leave to cool.

Pour the wine sauce over the pears and chill in the refrigerator for at least 3 hours before serving with whipped cream, if using.

4

makes about 675 g/1 lb 8 oz

450 g/1 lb Bramley apples, washed and
cut into chunks

600 ml/1 pint water

1 bottle red wine

about 675 g/1 lb 8 oz preserving sugar
(see method)

Wine jelly

Place the apples in a preserving pan together with the water and wine.
Bring to the boil, then reduce the heat and simmer for 30 minutes, or until
the apples are very soft and pulpy. Strain through a jelly bag.

Once all the juice has been extracted, measure and return to the
rinsed-out preserving pan. Add the sugar, allowing 450 g/1 lb of sugar
for every 600 ml/1 pint of juice. Heat gently, stirring frequently, until the
sugar has completely dissolved. Bring to the boil and boil rapidly for
15 minutes, or until the setting point is reached.

Leave to cool slightly, skim, then pot into warmed sterilized jars and
cover the tops with waxed discs. When completely cold, cover with
cellophane or lids, label and store in a cool place.

29. Vegetable Stock

serves 6

2 carrots, sliced

1 onion, diced

1 garlic clove, crushed

350 g/12 oz new potatoes, diced

2 celery sticks, sliced

400 g/14 oz canned chopped tomatoes

600 ml/1 pint vegetable stock

1 bay leaf

1 tsp dried mixed herbs or 1 tbsp chopped
    fresh mixed herbs

85 g/3 oz sweetcorn kernels, frozen or
    canned, drained

55 g/2 oz green cabbage, shredded

pepper

Chunky vegetable soup

Put the carrots, onion, garlic, potatoes, celery, tomatoes and stock into a large saucepan. Stir in the bay leaf and herbs. Bring to the boil, then reduce the heat, cover and simmer for 25 minutes.

Add the sweetcorn and cabbage and return to the boil. Reduce the heat, cover and simmer for 5 minutes, or until the vegetables are tender. Remove and discard the bay leaf. Season to taste with pepper.

Ladle into warmed soup bowls and serve immediately.

serves 8

350 g/12 oz lean pork fillet

1 tbsp vegetable oil

1 medium onion, chopped

2 garlic cloves, crushed

25 g/1 oz plain flour

2 tbsp tomato purée

425 ml/15 fl oz vegetable stock

125 g/4½ oz button mushrooms, sliced

1 large green pepper, deseeded and
    chopped

½ tsp freshly grated nutmeg

4 tbsp natural yogurt, plus extra to
    serve

salt and pepper

boiled rice, to serve

Pork stroganoff

Trim off any fat or gristle from the pork and cut into 1-cm/½-inch thick slices. Heat the vegetable oil in a large, heavy-based frying pan and gently fry the pork, onion and garlic for 4–5 minutes, or until lightly browned.

Stir in the flour and tomato purée, then pour in the vegetable stock and stir to mix thoroughly. Add the mushrooms, pepper, salt and pepper to taste and nutmeg. Bring to the boil, cover and simmer for 20 minutes, or until the pork is tender and cooked through.

Remove the frying pan from the heat and stir in the yogurt. Transfer the pork to 4 large serving plates and serve with boiled rice and an extra spoonful of yogurt.

3

serves 3–4

1 litre/1¾ pints vegetable stock
70 g/2½ oz butter
1 tbsp olive oil, plus extra for brushing
1 red onion, finely chopped
1 garlic clove, finely chopped
300 g/10½ oz risotto rice
150 ml/5 fl oz dry white wine
250 g/9 oz frozen baby broad beans
3 large boneless duck breasts, about
 450 g/1 lb in total
50 g/2 oz freshly grated Parmesan cheese
salt and pepper

Duck & broad bean risotto

Bring the stock to the boil in a saucepan, then reduce the heat and keep simmering gently over a low heat while you are cooking the risotto.

Meanwhile, heat 40 g/1½ oz of the butter and the oil in a deep saucepan over a medium heat until the butter has melted. Add the onion and garlic and fry for about 5 minutes, until softened but not browned. Reduce the heat, add the rice and mix to coat in oil and butter. Cook, stirring constantly, for 2–3 minutes, or until the grains are translucent. Add the wine and cook, stirring constantly, until it has reduced.

Gradually add the hot stock, a ladleful at a time. Stir constantly and add more liquid as the rice absorbs each addition. After about 15 minutes, stir in the broad beans. Cook for a further 5 minutes, or until all the liquid has been absorbed and the rice is creamy but still firm to the bite.

Meanwhile, brush a griddle or heavy-based frying pan with oil and heat. Put the duck breasts on the griddle and cook over a medium heat for about 15 minutes, turning several times and ensuring that the skin is browned and crispy. Remove from the griddle and slice thinly.

When the risotto is cooked, remove from the heat and stir in the duck and any juices, the Parmesan cheese and remaining butter. Season to taste with salt and pepper and serve immediately.

4

serves 4

225 g/8 oz dried haricot beans

2 tbsp olive oil

4–8 baby onions, halved

2 celery sticks, cut into 5-mm/¼-inch slices

225 g/8 oz baby carrots, scrubbed and halved if large

300 g/10½ oz new potatoes, scrubbed and halved, or quartered if large

850 ml–1.2 litres/1½–2 pints vegetable stock

1 fresh bouquet garni

1½–2 tbsp light soy sauce

85 g/3 oz baby sweetcorn

115 g/4 oz frozen or shelled fresh broad beans, thawed if frozen

½–1 savoy or spring (Primo) cabbage, about 225 g/8 oz

1½ tbsp cornflour

2 tbsp cold water

salt and pepper

55-85 g/2-3 oz freshly grated Parmesan cheese or mature Cheddar cheese, to serve

Spring stew

Pick over the haricot beans, rinse thoroughly, drain and put in a large bowl. Cover with plenty of cold water and leave to soak overnight. The next day, drain, put in a saucepan and cover with cold water. Bring to the boil and boil rapidly for 10 minutes, then drain and set aside.

Heat the oil in a large, heavy-based saucepan, with a tight-fitting lid, and cook the vegetables, stirring frequently, for 5 minutes, or until softened. Add the stock, drained beans, bouquet garni and soy sauce, then bring to the boil. Reduce the heat, cover and simmer for 12 minutes.

Add the baby sweetcorn and broad beans and season to taste with salt and pepper. Simmer for a further 3 minutes.

Meanwhile, discard the outer leaves and hard central core from the cabbage and shred the leaves. Add to the saucepan and simmer for a further 3–5 minutes, or until all the vegetables are tender.

Blend the cornflour with the water, stir into the saucepan and cook, stirring, for 4–6 minutes, or until the liquid has thickened. Serve the cheese separately, for stirring into the stew.

30. Chillies

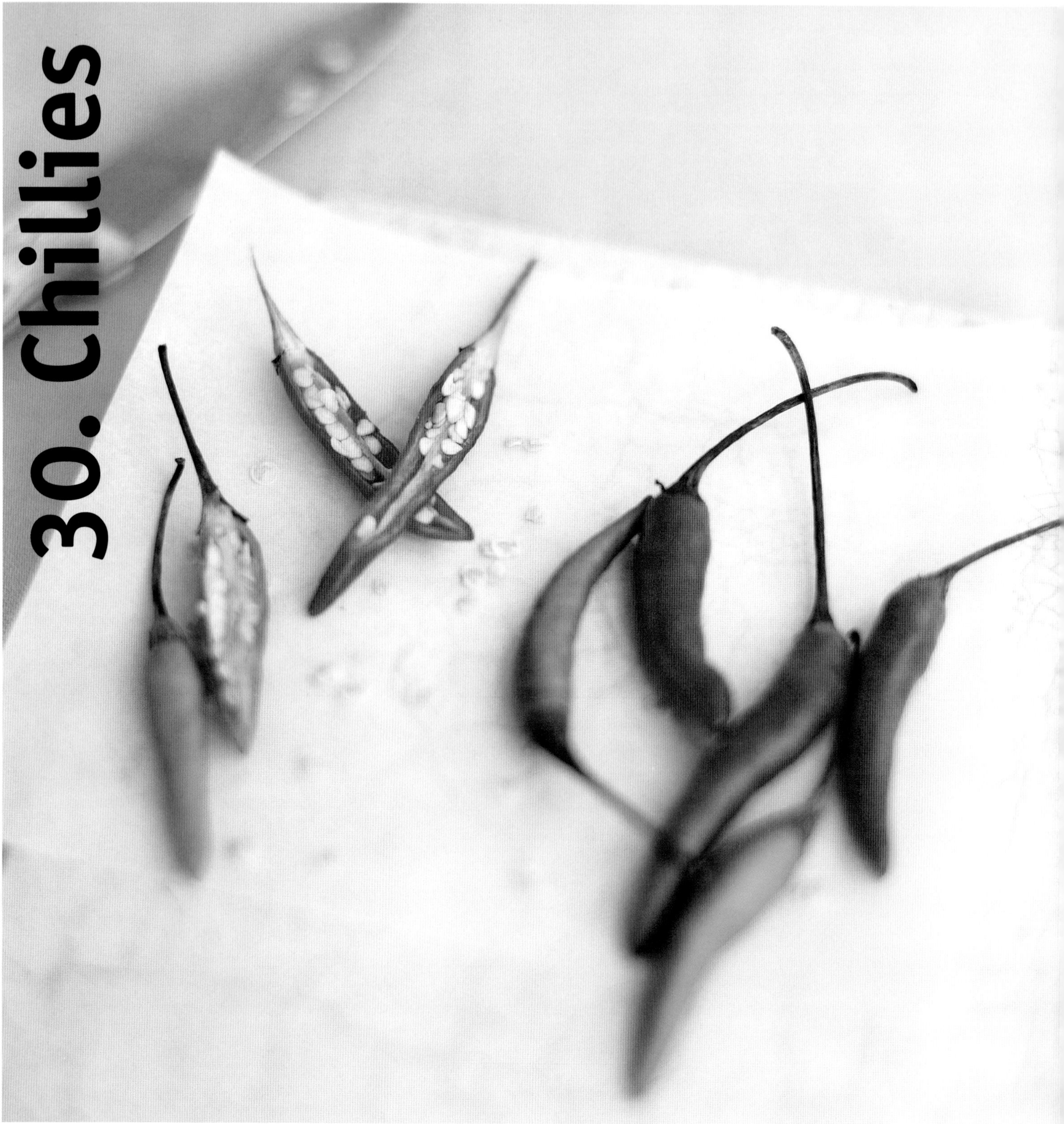

serves 6

4 tbsp sunflower oil

2 onions, chopped

1 garlic clove, chopped

1 tbsp plain flour

900 g/2 lb stewing steak, diced

300 ml/10 fl oz beef stock

300 ml/10 fl oz red wine

2–3 fresh red chillies, deseeded and
chopped

800 g/1 lb 12 oz canned red kidney beans,
drained and rinsed

400 g/14 oz canned chopped tomatoes

salt and pepper

tortilla chips, to serve

Chilli con carne

Heat half of the oil in a heavy-based saucepan. Add half the
chopped onion and the garlic and cook, stirring occasionally,
for 5 minutes, until softened. Remove with a slotted spoon.

Place the flour on a plate and season well with salt and pepper, then
toss the meat in the flour to coat. Cook the meat, in batches, until
browned all over, then return the meat and the onion mixture to the
saucepan. Pour in the stock and wine and bring to the boil, stirring.
Reduce the heat and simmer for 1 hour.

Meanwhile, heat the remaining oil in a frying pan. Add the remaining
onion and the chillies and cook, stirring occasionally, for 5 minutes.
Add the beans and tomatoes with their juice and break up with a
wooden spoon. Simmer for 25 minutes, until thickened.

Divide the meat between individual plates, top with the bean mixture
and serve with tortilla chips.

serves 4

500 g/1 lb 2 oz small new potatoes,
scrubbed

150 ml/5 fl oz vegetable oil

1 tsp chilli powder

1 fresh green chilli, deseeded and
finely chopped

½ tsp caraway seeds

1 tsp salt

shredded basil, for sprinkling

Chilli roast potatoes

Cook the potatoes in a saucepan of boiling water for 10 minutes, then
drain thoroughly.

Pour a little of the oil into a shallow roasting tin to coat the base. Heat the
oil in a preheated oven, 200°C/400°F/Gas Mark 6, for 10 minutes. Add
the potatoes to the tin and brush them with the hot oil.

In a small bowl, mix together the chilli powder, fresh chilli, caraway
seeds and salt. Sprinkle the mixture over the potatoes, turning to coat
them all over.

Add the remaining oil to the tin and roast in the oven for about
15 minutes, or until the potatoes are cooked through.

Using a slotted spoon, remove the potatoes from the the oil, draining
them thoroughly, and transfer them to a warmed serving dish. Sprinkle
the shredded basil over the top and serve immediately.

3

serves 4

2 tbsp sunflower oil

1 onion, chopped

1 garlic clove, finely chopped

1 tsp grated fresh ginger

1 tsp ground coriander

½ tsp chilli powder

¼ tsp ground turmeric

pinch of salt

350 g/12 oz fresh lamb mince

200 g/7 oz canned chopped tomatoes

1 tbsp chopped fresh mint

85 g/3 oz fresh or frozen peas

2 carrots, sliced into thin batons

1 fresh green chilli, deseeded and finely chopped

1 tbsp chopped fresh coriander

fresh mint sprigs, to garnish

crusty bread, to serve

Chilli lamb

Heat the oil in a large, heavy-based frying pan or flameproof casserole. Add the onion and cook over a low heat, stirring occasionally, for 10 minutes, or until golden.

Meanwhile, place the garlic, ginger, ground coriander, chilli powder, turmeric and salt in a small bowl and mix well. Add the spice mixture to the frying pan and cook, stirring constantly, for 2 minutes. Add the lamb and cook, stirring frequently, for 8–10 minutes, or until it is broken up and browned.

Add the tomatoes and their juices, the mint, peas, carrots, chilli and fresh coriander and cook, stirring constantly, for 3-5 minutes. Serve, garnished with fresh mint sprigs and some bread.

4

serves 4

tbsp curry paste	2 curry leaves
2 fresh green chillies, chopped	1 tsp ground cumin
5 dried red chillies	1 tsp ground coriander
2 tbsp tomato purée	½ tsp ground turmeric
2 garlic cloves, chopped	400 g/14 oz canned chopped tomatoes
1 tsp chilli powder	150 ml/5 fl oz chicken stock
pinch of sugar	4 skinless, boneless chicken breasts
pinch of salt	1 tsp garam masala
2 tbsp groundnut or sunflower oil	freshly cooked rice
½ tsp cumin seeds	fresh mint sprigs, to garnish
1 onion, chopped	

Red hot chilli chicken

To make the chilli paste, place the curry paste, fresh and dried chillies, tomato purée, garlic, chilli powder and sugar in a blender or food processor and add a pinch of salt. Process into a smooth paste.

Heat the oil in a large, heavy-based saucepan. Add the cumin seeds and cook over a medium heat, stirring constantly, for 2 minutes, or until they begin to pop and release their aroma. Add the onion and curry leaves and cook, stirring, for 5 minutes.

Add the chilli paste and cook for 2 minutes, then stir in the ground cumin, coriander and turmeric and cook for a further 2 minutes.

Add the tomatoes and their juices and the stock. Bring to the boil, then reduce the heat and simmer for 5 minutes. Add the chicken and garam masala, cover and simmer gently for 20 minutes, or until the chicken is cooked through and tender. Serve immediately with rice and garnished with fresh mint sprigs.

31. Curry Powder

1

serves 4

2 tsp butter

1 large onion, finely chopped

900 g/2 lb courgettes, sliced

450 ml/15 fl oz chicken or vegetable stock

1 tsp curry powder

125 ml/4 fl oz soured cream, plus extra to garnish

salt and pepper

Curried courgette soup

Melt the butter in a large saucepan over a medium heat. Add the onion and cook for about 3 minutes until it begins to soften.

Add the courgettes, stock and curry powder, along with a large pinch of salt, if using unsalted stock. Bring the soup to the boil, reduce the heat, cover and cook gently for about 25 minutes until the vegetables are tender.

Allow the soup to cool slightly, then transfer to a food processor or blender, working in batches if necessary. Process the soup until just smooth, but still with green flecks. (If using a food processor, strain off the cooking liquid and reserve. Process the soup solids with enough cooking liquid to moisten them, then combine with the remaining liquid.)

Return the soup to the rinsed-out saucepan and stir in the soured cream. Reheat gently over a low heat just until hot. (Do not boil.)

Taste and adjust the seasoning, if necessary. Ladle into warmed bowls, garnish with soured cream and serve.

2

serves 6

4 tbsp olive oil

900 g/2 lb skinless, boneless chicken, diced

125 g/4½ oz rindless smoked bacon, diced

12 shallots

2 garlic cloves, crushed

1 tbsp curry powder

300 ml/10 fl oz mayonnaise

1 tbsp clear honey

1 tbsp chopped fresh parsley

pepper

85 g/3 oz seedless white grapes, quartered, to garnish

cold saffron rice, to serve

Coronation chicken

Heat the oil in a large, heavy-based frying pan. Add the chicken, bacon, shallots, garlic and curry powder. Cook slowly, stirring, for about 15 minutes.

Spoon the mixture into a clean mixing bowl. Leave to cool completely, then season to taste with pepper.

Blend the mayonnaise with the honey, then add the parsley. Toss the chicken mixture in the mayonnaise mixture.

Place in a serving dish, garnish with the grapes and serve with cold saffron rice.

3

makes 24

115 g/4 oz plain flour, plus extra for dusting
pinch of salt
1 tsp curry powder
55 g/2 oz butter, plus extra for greasing
55 g/2 oz grated Cheddar cheese
1 egg, beaten
poppy and cumin seeds, for sprinkling

Cheese straws

Sift the flour, salt and curry powder into a bowl. Add the butter and
rub in until the mixture resembles breadcrumbs. Add the cheese and
half the egg and mix to form a dough. Wrap in clingfilm and chill in the
refrigerator for 30 minutes.

Preheat the oven to 200°C/400°F/Gas Mark 6, then grease several
baking trays. On a floured work surface, roll out the dough to 5 mm/
¼ inch thick. Cut into 7.5 x 1-cm/3 x ½-inch strips. Pinch the strips lightly
along the sides and place on the prepared baking trays.

Brush the strips with the remaining egg and sprinkle half with poppy
seeds and half with cumin seeds. Bake in the preheated oven for
10–15 minutes, or until golden. Transfer to wire racks to cool.

4

serves 4

4 ripe plantains
1 tsp curry powder
vegetable or groundnut oil, for deep-frying
mango chutney, to serve

Plantain chips

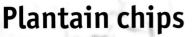

Peel the plantains, then cut crossways into 3-mm/⅛-inch slices. Put the slices in a bowl, sprinkle over the curry powder and use your hands to toss lightly together.

Heat enough oil for deep-frying in a wok, deep-fat fryer or large heavy-based saucepan to 180°C/350°F, or until a cube of bread browns in 30 seconds. Add as many plantain slices as will fit in the pan without overcrowding and fry for 2 minutes, or until golden.

Remove the plantain chips from the pan with a slotted spoon and drain well on crumpled kitchen paper. Serve hot with mango chutney.

32. Chorizo

serves 6

2 tbsp vegetable oil

500 g/1 lb 2 oz chicken breasts, cut into strips

250 g/9 oz chorizo, skinned and sliced

2 onions, chopped

4 garlic cloves, chopped

1 green pepper, deseeded and chopped

3 celery sticks, chopped

1 scotch bonnet chilli, carefully chopped

750 ml/1½ pints chicken stock

500 g/1 lb 2 oz long-grain rice

450 g/1 lb large cooked prawns or crayfish

cayenne pepper

salt

Jambalaya

Heat the oil in a large saucepan, then add the chicken and chorizo and brown for 5 minutes over a high heat. Reduce the heat and add the onions, garlic, green pepper and celery and sauté for a further 10 minutes, until soft. Add the chilli and the stock and stir in the rice. Cover and simmer very gently for 40 minutes.

Add the prawns and cook for a further 5 minutes. Check the seasoning, adding salt to taste. Serve.

serves 4

4 tbsp tomato purée

4 wholemeal or white muffins, halved

2 tbsp olives, stoned and chopped

3 button mushrooms, finely sliced

100 g/3½ oz chorizo, skinned and sliced

125 g/4½ oz mozzarella cheese, thinly sliced

Meat feast muffin pizzas

Spread the tomato purée over the cut sides of the halved muffins. Sprinkle over the olives, mushrooms and chorizo.

Lay the mozzarella slices over the toppings and place the muffins (about 4 halves at a time) in a large non-stick frying pan. Tightly cover with foil and place over a campfire or barbecue for 8–10 minutes, checking regularly to ensure that the base is not burning and the cheese is melting.

3

serves 4

125 g/4½ oz dried conchiglie

2 tbsp olive oil

1 medium onion, chopped

2 garlic cloves, very finely chopped

1 small yellow pepper, deseeded and cut into matchsticks

175 g/6 oz chorizo, skinned and sliced

2 tbsp red wine

1 tbsp red wine vinegar

125 g/4½ oz mixed salad leaves

salt

Chorizo & pasta salad

Bring a pan of lightly salted water to the boil over a medium heat. Add the pasta and cook for 8–10 minutes, or until tender but still firm to the bite. Drain thoroughly and reserve.

Heat the oil in a pan over a medium heat. Add the onion and cook until translucent. Stir in the garlic, yellow pepper and chorizo and cook for about 3–4 minutes, stirring once or twice.

Add the wine, vinegar and reserved pasta to the pan, stir and bring the mixture just to the boil over a medium heat.

Arrange the salad leaves on large serving plates, spoon over the warm chorizo and pasta mixture and serve immediately.

Serves 4

4 tbsp olive oil
2.25 kg/5 lb chicken, cut into
   8 pieces and dusted in flour
200 g/7 oz chorizo, skinned and sliced
small bunch of sage leaves
1 onion, chopped
6 garlic cloves, sliced
2 celery sticks, sliced
1 small pumpkin or butternut squash,
   peeled and roughly chopped
200 ml/7 fl oz dry sherry
600 ml/1 pint chicken stock
400 g/14 oz canned chopped tomatoes
2 bay leaves
salt and pepper
1 tbsp chopped fresh flat-leaf parsley

Chicken & chorizo casserole

Preheat the oven to 180°C/350°F/Gas Mark 4.

Heat the olive oil in a casserole, add the chicken, chorizo and sage
leaves and fry until golden brown. Remove with a slotted spoon and
reserve. You may need to do this in two batches.

Add the onion, garlic, celery and pumpkin to the casserole and cook for
20 minutes or until the mixture is golden brown.

Add the sherry, chicken stock, tomatoes and bay leaves, and season
with salt and pepper.

Put the reserved chicken, chorizo and sage back into the casserole dish.
Cover with a lid and cook in the oven for one hour.

Remove from the oven, stir in the chopped parsley and serve.

33. Cashew Nuts

serves 4

1½ tbsp groundnut oil

150 g/5½ oz mangetout

150 g/5½ oz baby sweetcorn

1 large orange or yellow pepper, deseeded and thinly sliced

8 spring onions, halved lengthways

2 garlic cloves, well crushed

2-cm/¾-inch piece fresh ginger, peeled and finely chopped

2 tbsp teriyaki marinade

100 g/3½ oz cashew nuts

400 g/14 oz large cooked peeled prawns

1 tbsp sesame oil

Teriyaki prawns with cashew nuts

Heat the groundnut oil in a large, non-stick preheated wok or frying pan, add all the vegetables and stir-fry over a high heat for 4 minutes, or until almost tender. Add the garlic and ginger and stir-fry for 1 minute.

Add the teriyaki marinade, cashew nuts and prawns and stir-fry for 2 minutes.

Serve immediately, with the sesame oil drizzled over.

serves 4

1 tbsp cornflour

½ tsp five-spice powder

4 turkey steaks, cut into thin strips

1 tsp soy sauce

1 tsp dry sherry

3 tbsp groundnut oil

1 garlic clove, finely chopped

2.5-cm/1-inch piece fresh ginger, finely chopped

4 spring onions, cut into thin strips

1 large carrot, cut into thin strips

85 g/3 oz cashew nuts

2 tbsp hoisin sauce

½ tsp salt

shredded spring onion, to garnish

cooked rice, to serve

Turkey & cashew nut stir-fry

Mix together the cornflour and five-spice powder in a bowl and stir in the turkey. Add the soy sauce and sherry, stirring to coat. Set aside for 30 minutes.

Heat a wok or large frying pan over a high heat. Heat 2 tablespoons of the oil, then add the turkey mixture and stir-fry for 2–3 minutes, until golden and cooked through. Using a slotted spoon, transfer the turkey to a plate and keep warm.

Heat the remaining oil in the wok and stir-fry the garlic, ginger, spring onions and carrot for 1 minute. Return the turkey to the wok with the cashew nuts, hoisin sauce and salt. Reduce the heat to medium–high and stir-fry for a further minute. Sprinkle with shredded spring onion and serve immediately with cooked rice.

3

serves 4

2 tbsp olive oil

1 tbsp butter

1 red onion, chopped

150 g/5½ oz arborio rice

1 tsp ground turmeric

1 tsp ground cumin

½ tsp chilli powder

3 garlic cloves, crushed

1 fresh green chilli, deseeded and sliced

1 green pepper, deseeded and diced

1 red pepper, deseeded and diced

85 g/3 oz baby sweetcorn, halved lengthways

2 tbsp stoned black olives

1 large tomato, deseeded and diced

450 ml/16 fl oz vegetable stock

85 g/3 oz cashew nuts

55 g/2 oz frozen peas

2 tbsp chopped fresh parsley

pinch of cayenne pepper

salt and pepper

Spicy cashew nut paella

Heat the oil and butter in a large frying pan or paella pan until the butter has melted.

Add the onion and cook over a medium heat, stirring constantly, for 2–3 minutes, until softened.

Stir in the rice, turmeric, cumin, chilli powder, garlic, chilli, green and red peppers, baby corn, olives and tomato and cook over a medium heat, stirring occasionally, for 1–2 minutes.

Pour in the stock and bring the mixture to the boil. Reduce the heat and cook gently, stirring constantly, for a further 20 minutes.

Add the cashew nuts and peas and continue to cook, stirring occasionally, for a further 5 minutes. Season to taste with salt and pepper and add the parsley and a pinch of cayenne pepper. Transfer the paella to warm serving plates and serve immediately.

serves 4

2 tbsp groundnut or vegetable oil

2 red onions, cut into wedges

1 small head cauliflower, cut into florets

1 small head broccoli, cut into florets

2 tbsp ready-made yellow curry paste or
    red curry paste

400 ml/14 fl oz canned coconut milk

1 tsp soy sauce

1 tsp granulated white sugar

1 tsp salt

85 g/3 oz cashew nuts

handful of fresh coriander, chopped, plus
    extra sprigs, torn, to garnish

Cauliflower, broccoli & cashew nut salad

Heat the oil in a preheated wok, add the onions and stir-fry over a medium–high heat for 3–4 minutes, until starting to brown. Add the cauliflower and broccoli and stir-fry for 1–2 minutes. Stir in the curry paste and stir-fry for 30 seconds, then add the coconut milk, soy sauce, sugar and salt. Bring gently to the boil, stirring occasionally, then reduce the heat and simmer gently for 3–4 minutes, until the vegetables are almost tender.

Meanwhile, heat a separate dry frying pan until hot, add the cashew nuts and cook, shaking the pan frequently, for 2–3 minutes, until lightly browned. Add to the stir-fry with the chopped coriander, stir well and serve immediately, garnished with the torn coriander sprigs.

34. Chocolate

serves 4

175 g/6 oz unsalted butter, softened,
   plus extra for greasing

175 g/6 oz golden caster sugar

3 eggs, beaten

3 tbsp golden syrup

40 g/1½ oz ground almonds

175 g/6 oz self-raising flour

pinch of salt

40 g/1½ oz cocoa powder

icing

225 g/8 oz plain chocolate, broken into pieces

55 g/2 oz dark muscovado sugar

225 g/8 oz unsalted butter, diced

5 tbsp evaporated milk

½ tsp vanilla extract

makes 12

225 g/8 oz butter, softened

140 g/5 oz caster sugar

1 egg yolk, lightly beaten

2 tsp vanilla extract

225 g/8 oz plain flour

55 g/2 oz cocoa powder

pinch of salt

85 g/3 oz milk chocolate chips

85 g/3 oz white chocolate chips

115 g/4 oz plain chocolate, roughly
   chopped

Chocolate fudge cake

Preheat the oven to 180°C/350°F/Gas Mark 4. Grease and line the
bases of two 20-cm/8-inch sandwich tins.

To make the icing, place the chocolate, muscovado sugar, butter,
evaporated milk and vanilla extract in a heavy-based saucepan.
Heat gently, stirring constantly, until melted. Pour into a bowl and
leave to cool. Cover and chill in the refrigerator for 1 hour, or until
spreadable.

For the cake, place the butter and caster sugar in a bowl and beat
together until light and fluffy. Gradually beat in the eggs. Stir in the
golden syrup and ground almonds. Sift the flour, salt and cocoa
powder into a separate bowl, then fold into the mixture. Add a little
water, if necessary, to make a dropping consistency.

Spoon the mixture into the prepared tins and bake in the preheated
oven for 30–35 minutes, or until springy to the touch and a skewer
inserted in the centre comes out clean.

Leave the cakes in the tins for 5 minutes, then turn out onto wire
racks to cool completely. When the cakes are cold, sandwich them
together with half the icing. Spread the remaining icing over the top
and sides of the cake, swirling it to give a frosted appearance.

Mega chip cookies

Preheat the oven to 190°C/375°F/Gas Mark 5. Line 2–3 baking trays with
baking paper.

Put the butter and sugar into a bowl and mix well with a wooden spoon,
then beat in the egg yolk and vanilla extract. Sift together the flour, cocoa
powder and salt into the mixture, add both kinds of chocolate chips and
stir until thoroughly combined.

Make 12 balls of the mixture, put them onto the prepared baking trays,
spaced well apart, and flatten slightly. Press the pieces of plain chocolate
into the cookies.

Bake in the preheated oven for 12–15 minutes. Leave to cool on the
baking trays for 5–10 minutes, then using a palette knife carefully transfer
to wire racks to cool completely.

3

Chocolate orange mousse cake

Preheat the oven to 180ºC/350ºF/Gas Mark 4. Cream the sugar and margarine together in a mixing bowl until pale and fluffy. Gradually add the eggs, beating well with a wooden spoon between each addition. Sift the flour, baking powder and cocoa powder together, fold half into the egg mixture, then fold in the remainder. Spoon the mixture into a greased and base-lined 23-cm/to 9-inch springform cake tin and level the surface with the back of a spoon. Bake in a preheated oven for 20 minutes or until risen and firm to the touch. Cool in the tin.

Meanwhile, melt the chocolate in a bowl placed over a saucepan of gently simmering water, making sure that the bottom of the bowl does not touch the water. Cool, then stir in the orange rind and juice and the egg yolks.

Whisk the egg whites in a large bowl until they form stiff peaks. Gently fold a large spoonful of the egg whites into the chocolate mixture, then fold in the remainder. Spoon the mixture on top of the cooked, cooled sponge and level the top with the back of a spoon. Place in the refrigerator to set. Remove the sides of the tin, then decorate with the orange rind strips and serve.

4

makes 9

115 g/4 oz butter, plus extra
   for greasing
115 g/4 oz plain chocolate, broken
   into pieces
300 g/10½ oz golden caster sugar
pinch of salt
1 tsp vanilla extract
2 large eggs
140 g/5 oz plain flour
2 tbsp cocoa powder
100 g/3½ oz white chocolate chips

fudge sauce

55 g/2 oz butter
225 g/8 oz golden caster sugar
150 ml/5 fl oz milk
250 ml/9 fl oz double cream
225 g/8 oz golden syrup
200 g/7 oz plain chocolate,
   broken into pieces

Double chocolate brownies

Preheat the oven to 180°C/350°F/Gas Mark 4. Grease an 18-cm/7-inch
square cake tin and line the base with baking paper.

Place the butter and chocolate in a small heatproof bowl set over a
saucepan of gently simmering water until melted. Stir until smooth, then
leave to cool slightly. Stir in the sugar, salt and vanilla extract. Add the
eggs, one at a time, and stir until blended.

Sift the flour and cocoa powder into the mixture and beat until smooth.
Stir in the chocolate chips, then pour the mixture into the prepared tin.
Bake in the preheated oven for 35–40 minutes, or until the top is evenly
coloured and a skewer inserted into the centre comes out almost clean.
Leave to cool slightly while you prepare the sauce.

To make the fudge sauce, place the butter, sugar, milk, cream and
golden syrup in a small saucepan and heat gently until the sugar has
dissolved. Bring to the boil and stir for 10 minutes, or until the mixture
is caramel-coloured. Remove from the heat and add the chocolate. Stir
until smooth. Cut the brownies into squares and serve immediately with
the sauce.

35. Maple Syrup

makes 10–12 slices

375 g/13 oz ready-made shortcrust pastry, thawed if frozen

60 g/2¼ oz plain flour, plus extra for rolling the pastry

3 tbsp soft light brown sugar

700 ml/1¼ pints double cream

250 ml/9 fl oz pure maple syrup

2 eggs

4 tsp lemon juice

½ tsp salt

½ tsp ground nutmeg

2 tbsp icing sugar

makes 16

175 g/6 oz unsalted butter, plus extra for greasing

115 g/4 oz plain chocolate

250 g/9 oz caster sugar

4 eggs, beaten

1 tsp vanilla extract

200 g/7 oz plain flour

85 g/3 oz pistachio nuts, chopped

glaze

115 g/4 oz plain chocolate

115 g/4 oz crème fraîche

2 tbsp maple syrup

Maple-cream tart

Preheat the oven to 200°C/400°F/Gas Mark 6. Roll out the pastry on a lightly floured surface and use to line a 23-cm/9-inch loose-based tart tin. Line the pastry with greaseproof paper and weigh down with dried beans. Place on a baking sheet and bake in the preheated oven for 15–20 minutes, until golden at the edges.

Meanwhile, combine the flour and sugar in a large bowl. Beat 450 ml/16 fl oz of the cream in another bowl with the maple syrup, eggs, lemon juice, salt and nutmeg. Slowly whisk this mixture into the flour, whisking until no lumps remain.

When the pastry case is golden, remove the paper and beans and reduce the oven temperature to 180°C/350°F/Gas Mark 4. Pour the filling into the pastry case, return to the oven and cook for 30–35 minutes, until set. Remove the tart from the oven and leave to cool completely on a wire rack.

Whip the remaining cream until soft peaks form. Sift over the icing sugar and continue whipping until stiff. Just before serving, spread the whipped cream over the surface of the tart. Cut into slices to serve.

Maple-glazed brownies

Preheat the oven to 190°C/375°F/Gas Mark 5. Lightly grease a 30 x 20-cm/12 x 8-inch shallow rectangular baking tin.

Place the butter and chocolate in a small pan over a very low heat and stir until melted. Remove from the heat.

Whisk the sugar, eggs and vanilla extract together in a large bowl until pale. Beat in the melted chocolate mixture. Sift in the flour evenly, then stir in 55 g/2 oz of the pistachio nuts.

Spoon into the prepared tin and smooth the surface. Bake in the preheated oven for 25–30 minutes, or until firm and golden brown.

For the glaze, melt the chocolate in a heatproof bowl set over a pan of gently simmering water. Stir in the crème fraîche and maple syrup and beat until smooth and glossy.

Spread the glaze evenly over the brownies with a palette knife. Sprinkle with the remaining pistachio nuts and leave until the topping is set. Remove from the tin and cut into squares.

3

makes 18

115 g/4 oz butter, softened, plus extra
   for greasing
85 g/3 oz pecan nuts
2 tbsp maple syrup
85 g/3 oz light muscovado sugar
1 large egg yolk, lightly beaten
115 g/4 oz self-raising flour

Pecan & maple biscuits

Preheat the oven to 190°C/375°F/Gas Mark 5. Lightly grease 2 baking trays. Reserve 18 pecan halves and roughly chop the rest.

Place the butter, maple syrup and sugar in a bowl and beat together with a wooden spoon until light and fluffy. Beat in the egg yolk. Sift over the flour and add the chopped pecan nuts. Mix to a stiff dough.

Place 18 spoonfuls of the mixture onto the baking trays, spaced well apart. Top each with a reserved pecan nut, pressing down gently.

Bake in the preheated oven for 10–12 minutes until light golden brown. Leave the cookies on the baking trays for 10 minutes then transfer to a cooling rack and leave to cool completely.

4

Serves 4–6

4 eggs

175 ml/6 fl oz milk

¼ tsp ground cinnamon

12 slices day-old challah or
  plain white bread

about 4 tbsp butter or margarine,
  plus extra to serve

½ –1 tbsp sunflower or corn oil

salt

warm maple syrup, to serve

French toast with
maple syrup

Preheat the oven to 140°C/275°F/Gas Mark 1. Break the eggs into a
large, shallow bowl and beat together with the milk, cinnamon and salt
to taste. Add the bread slices and press them down so that they are
covered on both sides with the egg mixture. Leave the bread to stand for
1–2 minutes to soak up the egg mixture, turning the slices over once.

Melt half the butter with ½ tablespoon of oil in a large frying pan. Add
to the pan as many bread slices as will fit in a single layer and cook for
2-3 minutes until golden.

Turn the bread slices over and cook until golden brown on the other
side. Transfer the French toast to a plate and keep warm in the oven
while cooking the remaining bread slices, adding extra oil and butter
if necessary.

Serve the French toast with the remaining butter melting on top and warm
maple syrup for pouring over.

36. Honey

serves 4

40 g/1½ oz butter

3 tbsp clear runny honey

500 g/1 lb 2 oz prepared winter squash
flesh (peeled and seeded weight),
cut into 2 cm/¾ in cubes

1 tsp finely chopped fresh thyme

salt and pepper

fresh thyme sprigs, to garnish

serves 4

about 175 g/6 oz goat's cheese, such
as Monte Enebro, in one piece

about 115 g/4 oz runny honey, such
as orange-blossom or thyme-
flavoured

100 g/3½ oz walnut halves, chopped

Honey-glazed sautéed squash

Put the butter and honey in a non-stick frying pan and heat gently
until melted. Add the squash cubes, chopped thyme and seasoning
and mix well. Sauté over a medium heat for about 8–10 minutes,
turning and tossing regularly, until the squash cubes are tender
and glazed all over (the glaze will gradually thicken and coat the
squash cubes).

Garnish with thyme sprigs and serve. Alternatively this dish can be
served as an accompaniment to a main meal.

Goat's cheese with honey & walnuts

Remove the cheese from the refrigerator at least 20 minutes before
serving to allow it to come to room temperature.

Pour the honey into a bowl. Place the walnuts in another bowl.

Serve the cheese on a board with a cheese knife and let everyone
cut a slice for themselves, drizzling over some honey, with a dipper,
if available, and sprinkling with chopped walnuts.

Alternatively, cut the cheese into quarters and place a portion on each
of 4 serving plates. Drizzle over some honey, sprinkle with chopped nuts
and serve.

3

serves 4

pasta

400 g/14 oz type 00 pasta flour
4 eggs, beaten
semolina, for dusting
salt

filling

400 g/1 lb 2 oz sweet potatoes
3 tbsp olive oil
1 large onion, finely chopped
1 garlic clove, crushed
1 tsp fresh thyme leaves, chopped
2 tbsp runny honey
salt and pepper

sage butter

50 g/1¾ oz butter
1 bunch fresh sage leaves finely
    chopped, reserving a few leaves
    for garnishing

Sweet potato ravioli

To make the pasta, sift the flour into a bowl or food processor. Add the eggs and combine to make a soft but not sticky dough. Dust a work surface with semolina and knead the dough for 4–5 minutes until smooth. Cover with clingfilm and refrigerate for at least 30 minutes.

For the filling, peel the sweet potatoes and cut into chunks. Cook in a saucepan of boiling water for 20 minutes, or until tender. Drain and mash.

Heat the oil in a frying pan over a medium heat, add the onion and cook for 4–5 minutes until softened but not coloured. Stir the onion into the mashed sweet potatoes and add the garlic and thyme. Drizzle with the honey and season to taste with salt and pepper. Set aside.

Using a pasta machine, roll the pasta out to a thickness of about 1 mm/¹⁄₃₂ inch (or use a rolling pin on a work surface lightly dusted with semolina). Cut the pasta in half. Place teaspoonfuls of the filling at evenly spaced intervals across one half of the pasta. Brush around the filling with water and cover with the second half of the pasta. Press lightly around the filling to seal the pasta and cut into squares with a sharp knife. Lay the ravioli out on a sheet of greaseproof paper that has been lightly dusted with semolina.

Bring a large saucepan of salted water to the boil and drop in the ravioli. Cook for 2–3 minutes until the pasta rises to the surface and is tender but still retaining a little bite.

Meanwhile, for the sage butter, melt the butter with the sage in a small saucepan over a gentle heat. Drain the ravioli and immediately toss with the sage butter. Serve immediately, garnished with sage leaves.

Serves 12–16

150 g/5½ oz unsalted butter, plus extra
  for greasing
115 g/4 oz light muscovado sugar
175 g/6 oz runny honey
1 tbsp lemon juice
2 eggs, beaten
200 g/7 oz self-raising flour
15 g/½ oz flaked almonds
warmed honey, to glaze

Honey & almond cake

Preheat the oven to 180°C/350°F/Gas Mark 4. Grease and line a 20-cm/
8-inch deep cake tin.

Place the butter, sugar, honey and lemon juice in a saucepan and stir
over a medium heat, without boiling, until melted and smooth.

Remove the pan from the heat and quickly beat in the eggs with a
wooden spoon. Sift in the flour and stir lightly with a metal spoon. Pour
into the prepared tin and scatter the almonds over the top.

Bake in the preheated oven for 35–40 minutes, until risen, firm and
golden brown. Cool in the tin for 15 minutes, then turn out onto a wire
rack to cool completely.

37. Raisins

serves 6–8

50 ml/2 fl oz red wine vinegar

25 g/1 oz caster sugar

1 bay leaf

pared rind of 1 lemon

150 g/5½ oz seedless raisins

4 large skinless, boneless chicken breasts, about 600 g/1 lb 5 oz in total

5 tbsp olive oil

1 garlic clove, finely chopped

150 g/5½ oz pine kernels

100 ml/3½ fl oz extra virgin olive oil

1 small bunch fresh flat-leaf parsley, finely chopped

salt and pepper

Chicken salad with raisins & pine kernels

To make the dressing, put the vinegar, sugar, bay leaf and lemon rind in a saucepan and bring to the boil, then remove from the heat. Stir in the raisins and leave to cool.

When the dressing is cool, slice the chicken breasts widthways into very thin slices. Heat the olive oil in a large frying pan, add the chicken slices and cook over a medium heat, stirring occasionally, for 8–10 minutes until lightly browned and tender.

Add the garlic and pine kernels and cook, stirring constantly and shaking the pan, for 1 minute or until the pine kernels are golden brown. Season to taste with salt and pepper.

Pour the cooled dressing into a large bowl, discarding the bay leaf and lemon rind. Add the extra virgin olive oil and whisk together. Season to taste with salt and pepper. Add the chicken mixture and parsley and toss together. Turn the salad into a serving dish and serve warm or, if serving cold, cover and chill in the refrigerator for 2–3 hours before serving.

serves 6

2 tbsp sunflower oil

2 onions, thinly sliced

2 eating apples, peeled, cored and thinly sliced

900 g/2 lb red cabbage, cored and shredded

4 tbsp red wine vinegar

2 tbsp sugar

¼ tsp ground cloves

55 g/2 oz raisins

125 ml/4 fl oz red wine

2 tbsp redcurrant jelly

salt and pepper

Braised red cabbage with raisins

Heat the oil in a large saucepan. Add the onions and cook, stirring occasionally, for 10 minutes, or until softened and golden. Stir in the apple slices and cook for 3 minutes.

Add the cabbage, vinegar, sugar, cloves, raisins and red wine and season to taste with salt and pepper. Bring to the boil, stirring occasionally. Reduce the heat, cover and cook, stirring occasionally, for 40 minutes, or until the cabbage is tender and most of the liquid has been absorbed.

Stir in the redcurrant jelly, transfer to a warmed dish and serve.

3

serves 6–8

225 g/8 oz unsalted butter,
  plus extra for greasing
225 g/8 oz plain chocolate
3 tbsp black coffee
55 g/2 oz soft light brown sugar
a few drops of vanilla extract
225 g/8 oz digestive biscuits, crushed
85 g/3 oz raisins
85 g/3 oz walnuts, chopped

No-bake chocolate cake

Grease and line a 450-g/1-lb loaf tin.

Place the chocolate, butter, coffee, sugar and vanilla extract in a saucepan over a low heat and stir until the chocolate and butter have melted, the sugar has dissolved and the mixture is well combined.

Add the crushed biscuits, the raisins and walnuts and stir well.

Spoon the mixture into the prepared loaf tin. Leave to set for 1–2 hours in the refrigerator, then turn out and cut into thin slices to serve.

Makes 12

250 g/9 oz rhubarb
125 g/4½ oz butter, melted and cooled
100 ml/3½ fl oz milk
2 eggs, beaten
200 g/7 oz plain flour
2 tsp baking powder
125 g/4 oz caster sugar
3 tbsp raisins
3 pieces stem ginger, chopped

Rhubarb & raisin muffins

Preheat the oven to 190°C/375°F/Gas Mark 5. Line a 12-cup muffin tin
with paper muffin cases.

Chop the rhubarb into lengths of about 1 cm/½ inch. Pour the melted
butter and milk into a large bowl and beat in the eggs. Sift the flour and
baking powder together and lightly fold into the wet mixture, together with
the sugar. Gently stir in the rhubarb, raisins and stem ginger.

Spoon the mixture into the muffin cases and bake in the preheated oven
for 15–20 minutes until the muffins are risen and golden and spring back
when gently touched in the centre with the tip of a forefinger. Serve warm.

38. Canned Tomatoes

1

serves 6

300 g/10½ oz sourdough bread

100 ml/3½ fl oz chicken stock

4 tbsp extra virgin olive oil

3 tbsp fresh sage leaves, shredded

4 garlic cloves, peeled and finely chopped

800 g/1 lb 12 oz canned chopped
tomatoes

1 tsp sugar

250 ml/9 fl oz hot water

55 g/2 oz freshly grated Parmesan cheese

salt and pepper

Italian tomato soup

Chop the bread into rough chunks, about 2.5 cm/1 inch square. Place a heavy-based saucepan over a medium heat. Add the stock, oil and sage and simmer until reduced by half. Add the bread and garlic, increase the heat to high and cook until all the liquid has been soaked up and the bread begins to crisp.

Add the tomatoes and sugar, stir and simmer for 15 minutes. Add up to 250 ml/9 fl oz hot water to thin the soup to your preferred consistency (it should be quite thick). Simmer for a further minute. Taste and adjust the seasoning.

Ladle into bowls, sprinkle a little Parmesan cheese on top and serve.

2

serves 4

2 tbsp olive oil

2 onions, chopped

2 garlic cloves, finely chopped

1 tbsp shredded fresh basil

800 g/1 lb 12 oz canned chopped
tomatoes

1 tbsp tomato purée

10–12 dried cannelloni tubes

butter, for greasing

225 g/8 oz ricotta cheese

115 g/4 oz cooked ham, diced

1 egg

55 g/2 oz freshly grated pecorino
cheese

salt and pepper

Ham & ricotta cannelloni

Preheat the oven to 180°C/350°F/Gas Mark 4. Heat the oil in a large heavy-based frying pan. Add the onions and garlic and cook over a low heat, stirring occasionally, for 5 minutes, or until the onion is softened. Add the basil, tomatoes and their can juices and tomato purée and season to taste with salt and pepper. Reduce the heat and simmer for 30 minutes, or until thickened.

Meanwhile, bring a large heavy-based saucepan of lightly salted water to the boil. Add the cannelloni tubes, return to the boil and cook for 8–10 minutes, or until tender but still firm to the bite. Using a slotted spoon, transfer the cannelloni tubes to a large plate and pat dry with kitchen paper.

Grease a large, shallow ovenproof dish with butter. Mix the ricotta, ham and egg together in a bowl and season to taste with salt and pepper. Using a teaspoon, fill the cannelloni tubes with the ricotta mixture and place in a single layer in the dish. Pour the tomato sauce over the cannelloni and sprinkle with the grated pecorino cheese. Bake in the preheated oven for 30 minutes, or until golden brown. Serve immediately.

3

serves 6

1.5 kg/3 lb 5 oz live mussels
3 tbsp olive oil
2 onions, chopped
3 garlic cloves, finely chopped
1 red pepper, deseeded and sliced
3 carrots, chopped
800 g/1 lb 12 oz canned chopped tomatoes
125 ml/4 fl oz dry white wine
2 tbsp tomato purée

1 tbsp chopped fresh dill
2 tbsp chopped fresh parsley
1 tbsp chopped fresh thyme
1 tbsp fresh basil leaves, plus extra to garnish
900 g/2 lb white fish fillets, cut into chunks
450 g/1 lb raw prawns
350 ml/12 fl oz fish stock or water
salt and pepper

Fishermen's stew

Clean the mussels by scrubbing or scraping the shells and pulling off any beards. Discard any with broken shells and any that refuse to close when tapped with a knife. Rinse the mussels under cold running water.

Heat the oil in a flameproof casserole. Add the onions, garlic, red pepper and carrots and cook over a low heat, stirring occasionally, for 5 minutes, or until softened.

Add the tomatoes and their juices, the white wine, tomato purée, dill, parsley and thyme, and tear in the basil leaves. Bring to the boil, then reduce the heat and simmer for 20 minutes.

Add the chunks of fish, mussels, prawns and stock and season to taste with salt and pepper. Return the stew to the boil and simmer for 6–8 minutes, or until the prawns have turned pink and the mussel shells have opened. Discard any shells that remain closed.

Serve immediately, garnished with basil leaves.

4

serves 4

pizza dough

450 g/1 lb plain flour, plus extra
    for dusting

2 tsp salt

2 tsp easy-blend dried yeast

2 tbsp olive oil, plus extra for
    brushing

6 fl oz lukewarm water

filling

2 tbsp olive oil

1 red onion, sliced thinly

1 garlic clove, chopped finely

400 g/14 oz canned chopped
    tomatoes

55 g/2 oz black olives, stoned

200 g/7 oz mozzarella cheese,
    drained and diced

1 tbsp chopped fresh oregano

salt and pepper

Calzone pizza turnover

To make the pizza dough, sift the flour and salt into a bowl and stir in the yeast. Make a well in the centre and pour in the oil and water. Gradually incorporate the dry ingredients into the liquid, using a wooden spoon or floured hands.

Turn out the dough onto a lightly floured surface and knead well for 5 minutes, or until smooth and elastic. Return to the clean bowl, cover with lightly oiled clingfilm and set aside to rise in a warm place for 1 hour, or until doubled in size. Meanwhile, preheat the oven to 200°C/400°F/Gas Mark 6. Heat the olive oil in a frying pan.

Add the onion and garlic and cook over a low heat, stirring occasionally, for 5 minutes, or until softened. Add the tomatoes and cook, stirring occasionally, for a further 5 minutes. Stir in the olives and season to taste with salt and pepper. Remove the frying pan from the heat.

Divide the dough into 4 pieces. Roll out each piece on a lightly floured surface to form a 20-cm/8-inch round.

Divide the tomato mixture among the rounds, spreading it over half of each almost to the edge. Top with the cheese and sprinkle with the oregano. Brush the edge of each round with a little water and fold over the uncovered sides. Press the edges to seal.

Transfer the turnovers to lightly oiled baking sheets and bake in the preheated oven for 15 minutes, or until golden and crisp. Remove from the oven and leave to stand for 2 minutes, then transfer to warmed plates and serve.

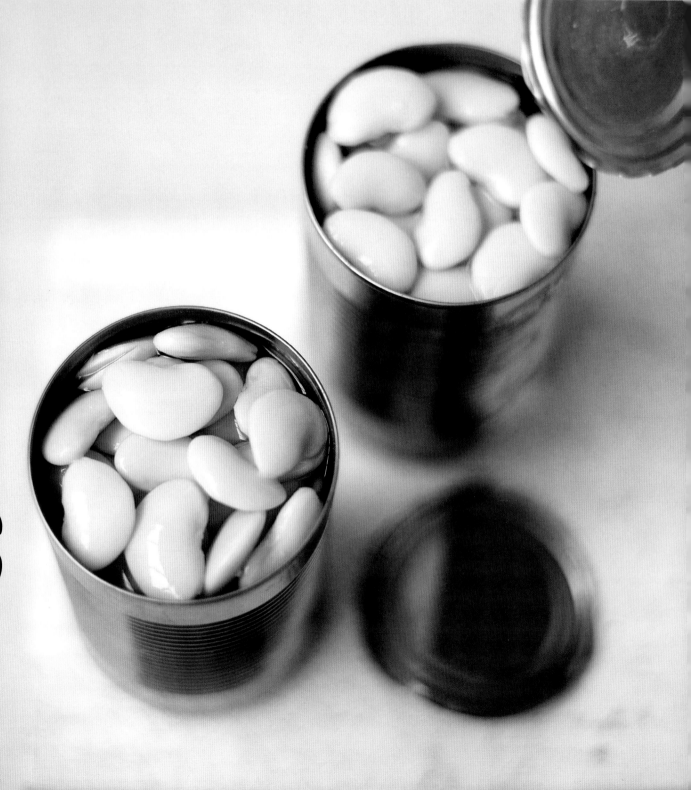

39. Butter Beans

1

serves 4

2 tbsp olive oil

1 onion, chopped

2 celery sticks, chopped

1 large carrot, roughly chopped

1 large or 2 small sweet potatoes, peeled and chopped

400 g/14 oz canned butter beans, drained and rinsed

1 litre/1½ pints vegetable stock

1 large handful fresh coriander leaves

2 tbsp freshly grated Parmesan cheese

salt and pepper

Sweet potato & butter bean soup

Heat the oil in a large saucepan over a medium heat, add the onion, celery and carrot and cook, stirring frequently, for 8–10 minutes, or until softened. Add the sweet potatoes and beans and cook, stirring, for 1 minute.

Add the stock, stir thoroughly and bring to a simmer. Season with a little salt and pepper to taste. Cover, reduce the heat and cook for 25–30 minutes until all the vegetables are tender.

Leave to cool slightly, then transfer one third of the soup to a blender or food processor and blend until smooth. Return to the saucepan and mix well. Check the seasoning and reheat.

Ladle into warmed bowls and scatter with the coriander and Parmesan cheese before serving.

2

serves 2

1 tbsp olive oil

1 small onion, finely diced

1 garlic clove, crushed

250 g/9 oz canned butter beans, drained and rinsed

90 ml/3 fl oz water

1 tbsp tomato purée

1 tsp balsamic vinegar

1 tbsp chopped fresh parsley

1 tbsp torn fresh basil

salt and pepper

slices of ciabatta bread, toasted, to serve

Tuscan beans on ciabatta toast with fresh herbs

Heat the oil in a medium sauté pan and cook the onion over a low heat until soft. Add the garlic and cook for a further 1 minute, then add the butter beans, water and tomato purée. Bring to the boil, stirring occasionally, and cook for 2 minutes.

Add the balsamic vinegar, parsley and basil and stir to combine. Season to taste with salt and pepper and serve over slices of toasted ciabatta.

3

serves 4

2 tbsp olive oil

1 tbsp fresh thyme, chopped

4 large sea bass fillets, about
  175 g/6 oz each

salt and pepper

cherry tomatoes on the vine, to serve

white bean purée

3 tbsp olive oil

2 garlic cloves, chopped

800 g/1 lb 12 oz canned butter beans,
  drained and rinsed

juice of 1 lemon

2–3 tbsp water

4 tbsp chopped fresh flat-leaf parsley

salt and pepper

Baked sea bass with white bean purée

Preheat the oven to 200°C/400°F/Gas Mark 6. Mix together the oil, thyme and a little salt and pepper to taste in a small bowl or jug. Arrange the sea bass fillets on a baking tray, pour over the oil mixture and carefully turn to coat well. Put the tray on the top shelf of the preheated oven and bake for 15 minutes.

Meanwhile, make the bean purée. Heat the oil in a saucepan over a medium heat, add the garlic and cook, stirring, for 1 minute. Add the beans and heat through for 3–4 minutes, then add the lemon juice and a little salt and pepper to taste. Transfer to a blender or food processor, add the water and blend lightly until you have a purée. Alternatively, mash thoroughly with a fork. Stir the parsley into the purée.

Spoon the purée onto 4 serving plates, lay the bass fillets on top and drizzle over any pan juices. Serve with vine tomatoes.

serves 4

1 large onion, peeled and chopped

125 g/4½ oz canned butter beans, drained and rinsed

125 g/4½ oz canned red kidney beans, drained and rinsed

125 g/4½ oz canned chickpeas, drained and rinsed

2 courgettes, roughly chopped

2 large carrots, roughly chopped

4 tomatoes, peeled and roughly chopped

2 celery sticks, trimmed and chopped

300 ml/10 fl oz vegetable stock

2 tbsp tomato purée

salt and pepper

crumble topping

85 g/3 oz wholemeal breadcrumbs

25 g/1 oz hazelnuts, very finely chopped

1 heaped tbsp chopped fresh parsley

115 g/4 oz Cheddar cheese, grated

Mixed bean & vegetable crumble

Preheat the oven to 180°C/350°F/Gas Mark 4.

Put the onion, butter beans, kidney beans, chickpeas, courgettes, carrots, tomatoes and celery in a large ovenproof dish. Mix together the stock and tomato purée and pour over the vegetables. Season to taste with salt and pepper. Transfer to the preheated oven and bake for 15 minutes.

Meanwhile, to make the crumble topping, put the breadcrumbs in a large bowl, add the hazelnuts, chopped parsley and grated cheese and mix together well.

Remove the vegetables from the oven and carefully sprinkle over the crumble topping. Do not press it down or it will sink into the vegetables.

Return the crumble to the oven and bake for 30 minutes, or until the crumble topping is golden brown. Remove from the oven and serve hot.

40. Canned Tuna

serves 4

1 x 30-cm/12-inch ready-made pizza base

3 tbsp red pesto

200 g/7 oz canned tuna in brine, drained

175 g/6 oz cherry tomatoes, halved

100 g/3½ oz mozzarella cheese, diced

2 tbsp capers

8 small black olives, stoned

1 tbsp olive oil

salt and pepper

makes 4 fishcakes

4 tbsp plain flour

200 g/7 oz canned tuna in brine, drained

2–3 tbsp curry paste

1 spring onion, trimmed and finely chopped

1 egg, beaten

sunflower or groundnut oil, for frying

salt and pepper

rocket leaves, to serve

Speedy tuna pizza

Preheat the oven to 220°C/425°F/Gas Mark 7. Place the pizza base on a baking tray, then spread the pesto evenly over the top.

Roughly flake the tuna and arrange over the pizza.

Scatter over the tomatoes, mozzarella, capers and olives. Season to taste with salt and pepper.

Drizzle the oil over the pizza and bake in the preheated oven for about 15 minutes, or until golden and bubbling.

Spicy tuna fishcakes

Mix the flour with plenty of salt and pepper on a large flat plate. Mash the tuna with the curry paste, spring onion and beaten egg in a large bowl.

Form into 4 patties and dust with the seasoned flour.

Heat the oil in a frying pan, add the patties and fry for 3–4 minutes on each side until crisp and golden. Serve on a bed of rocket leaves.

3

serves 4–6

200 g/7 oz dried ribbon egg pasta,
   such as tagliatelle

25 g/1 oz butter

55 g/2 oz fine fresh breadcrumbs

400 ml/14 fl oz canned condensed cream
   of mushroom soup

125 ml/4 fl oz milk

2 celery sticks, chopped

1 red pepper, deseeded and chopped

1 green pepper, deseeded and chopped

140 g/5 oz mature Cheddar cheese,
   coarsely grated

2 tbsp chopped fresh parsley

200 g/7 oz canned tuna in brine, drained
   and flaked

salt and pepper

Tuna & noodle casserole

Preheat the oven to 200°C/400°F/Gas Mark 6. Bring a large saucepan of salted water to the boil. Add the pasta, return to the boil and cook for 2 minutes less than specified on the packet instructions.

Meanwhile, melt the butter in a separate small saucepan. Stir in the breadcrumbs, then remove from the heat and set aside.

Drain the pasta well and set aside. Pour the soup into the pasta saucepan over a medium heat, then stir in the milk, celery, peppers, half the cheese and all the parsley. Add the tuna and gently stir in so that the flakes don't break up. Season to taste with salt and pepper. Heat just until small bubbles appear around the edge of the mixture – do not boil.

Stir the pasta into the saucepan and use 2 forks to mix all the ingredients together. Spoon the mixture into an ovenproof dish that is also suitable for serving and spread it out.

Stir the remaining cheese into the buttered breadcrumbs, then sprinkle over the top of the pasta mixture. Bake in the preheated oven for 20–25 minutes until the topping is golden. Remove from the oven, then leave to stand for 5 minutes before serving straight from the dish.

4

Serves 2

1 large egg, hard-boiled and cooled
200 g/7 oz canned tuna in brine, drained
200 g/7 oz canned sweetcorn kernels in
   water, drained
2 wholemeal flour tortillas
1 punnet mustard cress

Dressing
1 tbsp natural yogurt
1 tsp olive oil
½ tsp white wine vinegar
½ tsp Dijon mustard
pepper

Tuna, egg & sweetcorn wraps

To make the dressing, whisk the yogurt, oil, vinegar, mustard, and pepper
to taste, in a jug until emulsified and smooth.

Peel the egg, separate the yolk and the white, then mash the yolk and
finely chop the white. Mash the tuna with the egg and dressing, then mix
in the sweetcorn.

Spread the filling equally over the 2 tortillas and sprinkle over the mustard
cress. Fold in one end of each tortilla and roll up.

41. Black Olives

serves 4

a few vine leaves

4 tomatoes, sliced

½ cucumber, peeled and sliced

1 small red onion, thinly sliced

115 g/4 oz feta cheese, cubed

8 stoned black olives

dressing

3 tbsp extra virgin olive oil

1 tbsp lemon juice

½ tsp dried oregano

salt and pepper

serves 6–8

115 g/4 oz black olives in oil, drained and 2 tbsp oil reserved

140 g/5 oz butter, softened

4 tbsp fresh parsley, chopped

4 skinless, boneless chicken breasts

Greek feta salad

To make the dressing, put the oil, lemon juice, oregano and salt and pepper in a screw-top jar and shake together until blended.

Arrange the vine leaves on a serving dish and then the tomatoes, cucumber and onion. Scatter the cheese and olives on top. Pour the dressing over the salad and serve.

Chicken rolls with olives

Preheat the oven to 200°C/400°F/Gas Mark 6. Stone and finely chop the olives. Mix the olives, butter and parsley together in a bowl.

Place the chicken breasts between 2 sheets of clingfilm and beat gently with a meat mallet or the side of a rolling pin.

Spread the olive and herb butter over one side of each flattened chicken breast and roll up. Secure with a wooden cocktail stick or tie with clean string if necessary.

Place the chicken rolls in an ovenproof dish. Drizzle over the oil from the olive jar and bake in the preheated oven for 45–55 minutes, or until tender and the juices run clear when the chicken is pierced with the point of a sharp knife.

Transfer the chicken rolls to a chopping board and discard the cocktail sticks or string. Using a sharp knife, cut into slices, then transfer to warmed serving plates and serve.

3

makes 2 loaves

400 g/14 oz plain flour, plus extra
    for dusting
1 tsp salt
1 sachet easy-blend dried yeast
1 tsp brown sugar
1 tbsp chopped fresh thyme
200 ml/7 fl oz lukewarm water
4 tbsp olive oil, plus extra for brushing
55 g/2 oz black olives, stoned and sliced
55 g/2 oz green olives, stoned and sliced
100 g/3½ oz sun-dried tomatoes in oil,
    drained and sliced
1 egg yolk, beaten

Olive & sun-dried tomato bread

Sift the flour and salt together into a bowl and stir in the yeast, sugar and thyme. Make a well in the centre and pour in the lukewarm water and olive oil. Stir well with a wooden spoon until the dough begins to come together, then knead with your hands until it leaves the side of the bowl. Turn out on to a lightly floured surface and knead in the olives and sun-dried tomatoes, then knead for a further 5 minutes, until the dough is smooth and elastic.

Brush a bowl with oil. Shape the dough into a ball, put it in the bowl and put the bowl into a plastic bag or cover with a damp tea towel. Leave to rise in a warm place for 1–1½ hours, until the dough has doubled in volume.

Dust a baking sheet with flour. Turn out the dough onto a lightly floured surface and knock back. Cut it in half and with lightly floured hands, shape each half into a round or oval. Put them on the prepared baking sheet and put the baking sheet into a plastic bag or cover with a damp tea towel. Leave to rise in a warm place for 45 minutes.

Preheat the oven to 200°C/400°F/Gas Mark 6. Make 3 shallow diagonal slashes on the top of each loaf and brush with the beaten egg yolk. Bake for 40 minutes, until golden brown and the loaves sound hollow when tapped on the base with your knuckles. Transfer to a wire rack to cool.

4

serves 8

1.5 kg/3 lb 5 oz boned lamb shoulder, trimmed of fat and chopped into bite-sized cubes
4 tbsp olive oil
250 g/9 oz stoned dates
250 g/9 oz stoned black olives
700 ml/1¼ pints red wine
10 whole garlic cloves, peeled
large handful of coriander sprigs
couscous mixed with lemon zest and thyme leaves, to serve

dry marinade

2 large Spanish onions, grated
4 garlic cloves, crushed
1 red chilli, deseeded and finely chopped
1 tsp paprika
2 tsp ground cumin
1 tsp ground ginger
1 tsp pepper

Lamb tagine with dates & olives

Combine all the dry marinade ingredients in a casserole, add the lamb and leave to marinate in the refrigerator for 4 hours or overnight.

Preheat the oven to 150°C/300°F/Gas Mark 2. Remove the lamb from the refrigerator. Add all the remaining ingredients, except the coriander, to the casserole and cover. Transfer to the preheated oven and cook for 2½ hours, removing the lid for the last 30 minutes. Check that the lamb is meltingly tender, stir in the coriander and serve with couscous.

42. Onions

serves 6

3 tbsp olive oil

675 g/1 lb 8 oz onions, thinly sliced

4 garlic cloves, 3 chopped and 1 halved

1 tsp sugar

2 tsp chopped fresh thyme, plus extra
    sprigs to garnish

2 tbsp plain flour

125 ml/4 fl oz dry white wine

2 litres/3½ pints vegetable stock

6 slices French bread

300 g/10½ oz Gruyère cheese, grated

makes 12

140 g/5 oz besan or gram flour

1 tsp salt

1 tsp ground cumin

1 tsp ground turmeric

1 tsp bicarbonate of soda

½ tsp chilli powder

2 tsp lemon juice

2 tbsp vegetable or groundnut oil,
    plus extra for deep-frying

2–8 tbsp water

2 onions, thinly sliced

2 tsp coriander seeds, lightly crushed

French onion soup

Heat the oil in a large, heavy-based saucepan over a medium–low heat, add the onions and cook, stirring occasionally, for 10 minutes, or until they are just beginning to brown. Stir in the chopped garlic, sugar and chopped thyme, then reduce the heat and cook, stirring occasionally, for 30 minutes, or until the onions are golden brown.

Sprinkle in the flour and cook, stirring constantly, for 1–2 minutes. Stir in the wine. Gradually stir in the stock and bring to the boil, skimming off any scum that rises to the surface, then reduce the heat and simmer for 45 minutes.

Meanwhile, preheat the grill to medium. Toast the bread on both sides under the grill, then rub the toast with the cut edges of the halved garlic clove.

Ladle the soup into 6 flameproof bowls set on a baking tray. Float a piece of toast in each bowl and divide the grated cheese between them. Place under the grill for 2–3 minutes, or until the cheese has just melted. Garnish with thyme sprigs and serve at once.

Onion bhaji

Sift the besan flour, salt, cumin, turmeric, bicarbonate of soda and chilli powder into a large bowl. Add the lemon juice and the oil, then very gradually stir in just enough water until a batter similar in consistency to single cream forms. Mix in the onions and coriander seeds.

Heat enough oil for deep-frying in a wok, deep-fat fryer or large, heavy-based saucepan until it reaches 180°C/350°F, or until a cube of bread browns in 30 seconds. Without overcrowding the pan, drop in spoonfuls of the onion mixture and fry for 2 minutes, then use tongs to flip the bhajis over and continue frying for a further 2 minutes, or until golden brown.

Immediately remove the bhajis from the oil and drain well on crumpled kitchen paper. Keep the bhajis warm while you continue frying the remaining batter. Serve hot.

3

serves 4–6

100 g/3½ oz unsalted butter

600 g/1 lb 5 oz onions, thinly sliced

2 eggs

100 ml/3½ fl oz double cream

100 g/3½ oz grated Gruyère cheese

20-cm/8-inch ready-baked pastry case

100 g/3½ oz Parmesan cheese, coarsely grated

salt and pepper

Caramelized onion tart

Melt the butter in a heavy-based frying pan over a medium heat. Add the onions and cook, stirring frequently to avoid burning, for 30 minutes, or until well-browned and caramelized. Remove the onions from the pan and set aside.

Preheat the oven to 190°C/375°F/Gas Mark 5. Beat the eggs in a large bowl, stir in the cream and season to taste with salt and pepper. Add the Gruyère cheese and mix well. Stir in the cooked onions.

Pour the egg and onion mixture into the baked pastry case and sprinkle with the Parmesan cheese. Place on a baking tray and bake in the preheated oven for 15–20 minutes until the filling has set and is beginning to brown.

Remove from the oven and leave to rest for at least 10 minutes. The tart can be served hot or left to cool to room temperature.

4

Serves 4

450 g/1 lb floury potatoes
1 medium onion, grated
salt and pepper
oil, for shallow frying

Onion rösti

Wash the potatoes, but do not peel them. Place in a large saucepan, cover with water and bring to the boil, covered, over a high heat. Reduce the heat and simmer for about 10 minutes, until the potatoes are just beginning to soften. Be careful not to overcook.

Drain the potatoes. Leave to cool, then peel them and grate coarsely. Mix the grated onion with the potatoes. Season the mixture with salt and pepper.

Heat the oil in a heavy-based frying pan and spoon in the potato mixture. The rösti can be as thick or as thin as you like, and the mixture can be made into one large cake or several individual ones.

Cook over a high heat for about 5 minutes, until the bottom is golden, then turn and cook until the second side is brown and crispy. Remove from the heat, drain and serve.

serves 6

1 kg/2 lb potatoes

150 g/5½ oz butter, plus extra for greasing

500 ml/17 fl oz milk

600 g/1 lb 5 oz firm white fish fillets, such as cod, haddock or pollack

400 g/14 oz undyed smoked haddock fillet

3 bay leaves

55 g/2 oz plain flour

handful of fresh parsley, chopped

250 g/9 oz cooked peeled prawns

4 hard-boiled eggs, shelled and quartered

55 g/2 oz melted butter, plus extra for greasing

salt and pepper

minted peas and crusty french baguette, to serve

Fish pie

Peel and quarter the potatoes. Bring a large saucepan of lightly salted water to the boil, add the potatoes and cook for 15–20 minutes, or until tender. Drain, mash thoroughly with half of the butter and 2 tablespoons of the milk, then season with salt and pepper, cover and keep warm.

Place the fish fillets in a shallow saucepan and pour over the remaining milk. Add the bay leaves and place over a low heat. Bring the milk to a gentle simmer and poach the fish for 4 minutes (the fillets should not be fully cooked as they will be baked later). Remove from the saucepan and place on a plate, discard the bay leaves and reserve the milk. Remove any remaining bones and skin from the fish and flake into large chunks. Put in a bowl, cover and set aside.

Melt the remaining butter in a saucepan, then stir in the flour to make a roux and cook, stirring occasionally, for 3 minutes. Gradually add the reserved milk, a ladleful at a time, and mix into the roux. Add the parsley, the fish, the prawns and the eggs. Fold carefully together. Season to taste with salt and pepper.

Preheat the oven to 200°C/400°F/Gas Mark 6. Grease a pie dish with butter and fill it with the fish mixture. Place the potatoes on top, making a pattern. Drip the melted butter over the whole pie, place in the oven and bake for 30–40 minutes until the top is golden brown.

Serve the pie with minted peas and some crusty French baguette.

serves 6

butter, for greasing

750 g/1 lb 10 oz potatoes, peeled and thinly sliced

2 spring onions, finely chopped

1 red onion, finely chopped

150 ml/5 fl oz double cream

500 g/1 lb 2 oz fresh ready-made puff pastry

2 eggs, beaten

salt and pepper

Potato & red onion pie

Preheat the oven to 200°C/400°F/Gas Mark 6. Lightly grease a baking tray. Bring a saucepan of water to the boil, add the sliced potatoes, bring back to the boil and then simmer for a few minutes. Drain the potato slices and leave to cool. Dry off any excess moisture with kitchen paper.

In a bowl, mix together the spring onions, red onion and the cooled potato slices. Stir in 2 tbsp of the cream and plenty of seasoning.

Divide the pastry in half and roll out one piece to a 23-cm/9-inch round. Roll the remaining pastry to a 25-cm/10-inch round.

Place the smaller circle on the baking tray and top with the potato mixture, leaving a 2.5-cm/1-inch border. Brush this border with a little of the beaten egg.

Top with the larger circle of pastry, seal well and crimp the edges of the pastry. Cut a steam vent in the middle of the pastry and, using the back of a knife, mark with a pattern. Brush with some of the beaten egg and bake in the preheated oven for 30 minutes.

Mix the remaining beaten egg with the rest of the cream and pour into the pie through the steam vent. Return to the oven for 15 minutes, then leave to cool for 30 minutes. Serve warm or cold.

3

serves 4

4 large potatoes, pricked with a fork
250 g/9 oz cooked chicken, diced
4 spring onions, thickly sliced
250 g/9 oz low-fat soft cheese
pepper
mixed salad, to serve

Baked potatoes with chicken

Preheat the oven to 200°C/400°F/Gas Mark 6. Bake the potatoes in the preheated oven for about 60 minutes, until tender, or cook in a microwave on high power for 12–15 minutes.

Mix the chicken and spring onions with the low-fat soft cheese.

Cut a cross through the top of each potato and squeeze slightly apart. Spoon the chicken filling into the potatoes and season to taste with pepper. Serve with a mixed salad.

Serves 4

1 kg/2 lb 4 oz potatoes
6 tbsp olive oil
2 sprigs fresh rosemary
150 g/5½ oz baby shallots
2 garlic cloves, sliced
salt and pepper

Roasted potato wedges with shallots & rosemary

Preheat the oven to 200°C/400°F/Gas Mark 6. Peel and cut each potato into 8 thick wedges. Put the potatoes in a large saucepan of lightly salted water and bring to the boil. Reduce the heat and simmer for 5 minutes.

Heat the oil in a large roasting tin. Drain the potatoes well and add to the roasting tin. Strip the leaves from the rosemary sprigs, chop finely and sprinkle over the potatoes.

Roast the potatoes in the preheated oven for 35 minutes, turning twice during cooking. Add the shallots and garlic and roast for a further 15 minutes until golden brown. Season to taste with salt and pepper.

Transfer to a warmed serving dish and serve hot.

44. Apples

1

serves 6

1 tbsp butter

3 leeks, thinly sliced

1 large carrot, thinly sliced

600 g/1 lb 5 oz sweet potatoes, peeled and diced

2 apples, peeled and sliced

1.2 litres/2 pints water

freshly grated nutmeg

225 ml/8 fl oz apple juice

225 ml/8 fl oz single cream

salt and pepper

snipped fresh chives or coriander, to garnish

Sweet potato & apple soup

Melt the butter in a large saucepan over a medium–low heat. Add the leeks, cover and cook for 6–8 minutes, or until soft, stirring frequently.

Add the carrot, sweet potatoes, apples and water. Season lightly with salt, pepper and nutmeg to taste. Bring to the boil, reduce the heat and simmer, covered, for about 20 minutes, stirring occasionally, until the vegetables are very tender.

Allow the soup to cool slightly, then transfer to a blender or food processor and purée until smooth, working in batches if necessary. (If using a food processor, strain off the cooking liquid and reserve. Purée the soup solids with enough cooking liquid to moisten them, then combine with the remaining liquid.)

Return the puréed soup to the saucepan and stir in the apple juice. Place over a low heat and simmer for about 10 minutes, until heated through.

Stir in the cream and continue simmering for about 5 minutes, stirring frequently, until heated through. Taste and adjust the seasoning, adding more salt, pepper and nutmeg, if necessary. Ladle the soup into warmed bowls, garnish with chives or coriander and serve.

2

serves 4

2 large lettuces

250 g/9 oz dried penne

8 apples, diced

juice of 4 lemons

1 head of celery, sliced

115 g/4 oz walnut halves

250 ml/9 fl oz fresh garlic mayonnaise

salt and pepper

Penne & apple salad

Wash and drain the lettuce leaves, then pat them dry with kitchen paper. Transfer them to the refrigerator for 1 hour, or until crisp.

Meanwhile, bring a large saucepan of lightly salted water to the boil. Add the pasta, bring back to the boil and cook for 8–10 minutes, or until tender but still firm to the bite. Drain the pasta and refresh under cold running water. Drain thoroughly and cool.

Core and dice the apples, place them in a bowl and sprinkle with the lemon juice to coat them thoroughly – this will prevent discoloration. Mix together the cooled pasta, celery, apples and walnut halves and toss the mixture in the garlic mayonnaise. Season to taste with salt and pepper.

Line a salad bowl with the lettuce leaves and spoon the pasta salad on top. Refrigerate until ready to serve.

3

makes about 3.5 kg/7 lb 10 oz

900 g/2 lb apples, peeled, cored and
  chopped

450 g/1 lb onions, chopped

450 g/1 lb ripe plums, rinsed,
  stoned and chopped

rind and juice of 2 lemons (preferably
  unwaxed and organic), scrubbed

225 g/8 oz fresh cranberries (if fresh are
  unavailable, use dried)

450 g/1 lb soft brown sugar

4 kiwi fruit, peeled and sliced

450 ml/16 fl oz malt vinegar

2 tbsp balsamic vinegar

Fruity apple chutney

Place the apples, onions and plums in a preserving pan with the lemon
rind, juice and cranberries. Cook over a gentle heat, stirring frequently,
for 12 minutes, or until the cranberries are beginning to 'pop'.

Stir in all the remaining ingredients and heat gently, stirring occasionally,
until the sugar has completely dissolved. Bring to the boil, then
reduce the heat and simmer for 35–40 minutes, or until a thick
consistency is reached.

Remove from the heat, leave to cool slightly then pot into warmed
sterilized jars. Cover with non-metallic lids, label and store in a
cool place.

0 g/1¾ oz plain flour

0 g/1¾ oz cornflour

inch of salt

tsp baking powder

egg

50 ml/5 fl oz iced water

apples, cored and sliced

olive or sunflower oil, for deep-frying

caster sugar, for dusting

ice cream, to serve

Hot apple fritters

Sift the flour, cornflour, salt and baking powder together into a large bowl. Stir in the egg and water and mix to a fairly smooth batter.

Heat the oil in a deep-fat fryer to 180–190°C/350–375°F, or until a cube of bread browns in 30 seconds. Dip the apple slices into the batter, add to the hot oil and cook until crisp and golden. Remove with a slotted spoon and drain on kitchen paper.

Dust the apple fritters with caster sugar and serve immediately with ice cream.

192